Recollections

of

Admiral Arleigh A. Burke,
U. S. Navy (Retired)

Years - 1955 - 1961.

U. S. Naval Institute
Annapolis, Maryland
1973.

Preface

Four interviews with Admiral Arleigh A. Burke, U. S. Navy (Retired), are included in this volume. They were obtained by John T. Mason, Jr., for the Oral History Program of the U. S. Naval Institute and with special permission to make a copy available to the Columbia University Oral History project on the Eisenhower Administration, and the Eisenhower Presidential Library in Abilene, Kansas.

These interviews cover largely the period from 1955 to 1961 when Admiral Burke served as Chief of Naval Operations and during which time he maintained a close relationship with President Eisenhower.

It is noted that Admiral Burke says little here about the Polaris project which was generated during the period. The Admiral's recollections of that project are covered elsewhere in an interview for the Naval Institute.

These interviews were given by Admiral Burke in a period of time ranging from November 1972 to January 1973. He saw the transcript of the tapes and has made a few minor changes and corrections. Subsequently the MS has been re-typed.

A subject index is affixed for the convenience of the user.

DECLARATION OF TRUST

The undersigned does hereby appoint and designate as his (her) Trustee herein, the Secretary-Treasurer and Publisher of the United States Naval Institute to perform and discharge the following duties, powers, and privileges in connection with the possession and use of a certain taped interview between the undersigned and the Oral History Department of the United States Naval Institute.

1. Classification of Transcript.

   ( )a. If classified <u>OPEN</u>, the transcript(s) may be read or the recording(s) audited by the qualified personnel upon presentation of proper credentials, as determined by the Secretary-Treasurer of the U. S. Naval Institute.

   (✓)b. If classified <u>PERMISSION REQUIRED TO CITE OR QUOTE</u>, the user will be required to obtain permission in writing from the interviewee prior to quoting or citing from either the transcript(s) or the recording(s).

   ( )c. If classified <u>PERMISSION REQUIRED</u>, permission must be obtained in writing from the interviewee before the transcribed interview(s) can be examined or the tape recording(s) audited.

   ( )d. If classified <u>CLOSED</u>, the transcribed interview(s) and the tape recording(s) will be sealed until a time specified by the interviewee. This may be until the death of the interviewee or for any specified number of years.

2. It is expressly understood that in giving this authorization, I am in no way precluded from placing such restrictions as I may desire upon use of the interview at any time during my lifetime, nor does this authorization in any way affect my rights to the copyright of my literary expressions that may be contained in the interview.

Witness my hand and seal this 7th day of May 19 73.

Arleigh Burke

I hereby accept and consent to the foregoing Declaration of Trust and the powers therein conferred upon me as Trustee:

R. E. Bowker Jr.

Interview with Admiral Arleigh Burke   November 14, 1972
by John T. Mason, Jr.   Washington, D. C.

Q: This is an interview on the Admiral's relationship in a personal way and an official way with General Eisenhower, during the years of the General's Presidency, 1953-61.

Your naval career has been so tremendous and so significant to the Navy and the nation, I do hope that someone will do an adequate biography of you some time. You're known affectionately by many of your friends and admirers as "Mr. Navy" and I think that is truly significant as a name. However, today I would ask you to focus on your relationship with General Eisenhower. I wonder if you'd begin by telling me about your very first meeting with him?

Admiral Burke: Well, first I want to thank you for those very kind and generous words. But biographies of military men aren't very popular these days.

I think the very first time I ever met President Eisenhower was when he was president of Columbia University. He was appointed by the President to investigate and advise on the Defense Department before there was a Defense Department. He was a sort of a predecessor of the Secretary of Defense, and he came down and was briefed by all the services on their war plans, what they were supposed to do--well, the whole attitude of the services and everything else.

I remember that I was told--I was given the task of briefing him on the use of carriers, because he didn't know anything about carriers. He had a lot of beliefs about them but he didn't really know. I don't think he had ever seen a carrier operate.

Q: What was your position at that time?

Burke: I think I was the Navy's planner. I'm sure I was the Navy Planner, I think it was Op-30 at that time.

I arranged a briefing using slides and charts and all the other props that I could use, and some movies in places. When I went into the briefing, in to brief him, the first one was in a room adjacent to the CNO's office, and I stood up at a podium, on a podium in that little room, and he was a one man audience. There was nobody else there. And I never before had to give a speech or a briefing to one man. It was a very difficult position for me, because I realized that the effectiveness of that briefing might have great impact on the Navy in the future, so I wanted to do a good job.

But he was very kind. He listened. He didn't know anything at all about warfare at sea. He knew about warfare of movement but I don't think he ever did get out of his general's mind, corps boundaries, and why they couldn't be applied--he never understood why corps boundaries or something similar to that could not be applied to sea warfare.

Q: That's curious, Admiral, because he'd had service in the Philippines, a group of islands surrounded by water and dependent upon the Navy.

Burke: He had, he had, but he had looked upon the Navy and upon the oceans as some way of getting an Army from here to there. Transportation. It was transportation outfit. And he didn't really understand it, so I explained in detail how carriers operated, why they operated the way they did, why they moved so far and so fast, the difficulties of operating carriers, the vulnerabilities of carriers, and also the effectiveness of the carriers during the war.

I had some movies. I showed him the movies. I showed him slides and charts and everything else that I could think of. I don't know how long this lasted, but perhaps two days. He asked a lot of penetrating questions, questions that you would expect an Army officer to ask, and they were good questions. Why was it really necessary? Why couldn't you get more aircraft on carriers? Why was the mix of aircraft the way it was? Why did you have to have all of those ships with carriers? The carrier task force. The whole gamut of questions.

And he hoisted it aboard pretty well, but there were some things that years later I found I had not done a very good job on. One of them was that naval forces had to do a multiple of jobs--that is, a destroyer, a single ship, had to be capable of not only one task but many tasks, and the Army didn't operate that way, couldn't operate that way. It was a different type of service.

Another one, the boundary business, there are no boundaries at sea. There are no natural separations. Well, there are a few, but usually in the high seas there are no natural separations, and so the command setup had to be a lot different and a lot more flexible that the Army command system.

But he was a very fine man.

Q: You really succeeded in putting across the concept of the airplane and the Navy?

Burke: I succeeded partly anyway, but I don't think it was wholly a success, I found out later, at times. But he was a very fine man.

I'd heard a lot of stories about General Eisenhower

before, and some of them weren't very pleasant. I mean, the fact that he was a compromiser, that he didn't really run the Army in Europe, that he was just a sort of a political head--a lot of other stories that detracted from his reputation. But I commenced to admire him, because he really dug into the questions of the Navy. He did not do a superficial job.

Q: He'd done some homework.

Burke: He did his homework, that's right. I don't know when that was. That was probably maybe around '52 or '53.

Q: It must have been earlier than that.

Burke: Oh yes, it must have been. It must have been.

Q: '50, '51 . . .

Burke: Yes, '51, I guess.

Q: Well, that was an interesting experience and you say it went on two whole days. Did anybody join you?

Burke: Sometimes--who was CNO then?

Q: Admiral Sherman was Chief of Naval Operations. After that presentation, you didn't see him again?

Burke: No. I don't think so. I saw him, but I mean I never talked to him until after he was elected President, or until I was appointed CNO.

Q: As an active duty Navy man you weren't particularly concerned about his election initially to the Presidency?

Burke: No. I thought he was a good man and I voted for him, but many times I didn't vote when I was on active duty but this time I did because I knew him and thought he was a good man.

Q: So your first real relationship after that briefing came when you were designated as Chief of Naval Operations.

Burke: Yes. And by that time, he had forgotten he'd ever seen me, because when the Secretary of Defense and the Secretary of the Navy, (and I guess the Deputy Secretary of Defense) went over to see President Eisenhower to suggest that I be appointed . . .

Q: This was after it was determined that Carney was stepping down?

Burke: No, it was before. It was before. I think it was while they were determining what should be done, they recommended me, probably because when it was suggested that

Admiral Carney would step down, of course they would ask, who would replace him? And they recommended me. I wasn't there, of course, but Mr. Thomas says that when he did this, President Eisenhower said, "Who's he?"

"Never heard of him."

Well, they explained and then the President said, "Well, if you think he's the best man and you've studied it, why, I'll go along." But he did not know me. He was a little reluctant because I was young and junior.

Q: It meant reaching far down.

Burke: It meant reaching far down. It meant upsetting a lot of things, and he knew what that meant in the service and he didn't like that very much, but he went along with it. But I was not his choice. He didn't have any choice.

Q: Had you known Secretary Wilson?

Burke: No, neither Wilson nor Thomas. Gates I knew a little bit. He was Under Secretary of the Navy at that time.

Q: So you got named, of course.

Burke: I got named. The next time I saw him was when I

Burke 1 - 8

went over with Mr. Wilson and Mr. Thomas for the President to see me before he appointed me, after everything had been set up. There was no question, if I didn't stub my toe he was going to appoint me. That was the next time I saw him.

Q: Then you had to go before the Congressional committee.

Burke: Yes, right after that. I don't remember much about that. I think it was sort of a pro forma business.

Q: I would think it would be, based on your reputation.

Burke: No, no. No. I should not have been appointed. I think I said in a previous interview, I should not have been appointed CNO and I objected to it at the time because it was upsetting and I would have been a better Chief if I had had a couple of years in other jobs in a more senior position, and if I'd been a little bit older and a little bit more experienced. I always believed that, even when I was promoted during the war, Admiral Mitscher one time, for whom I was chief of staff, recommended me for promotion to rear admiral. There were a few being promoted ahead of time. And he had some personal correspondence with Admiral Nimitz or maybe talked to him about it, I don't know, and so he wrote a personal letter to Admiral Nimitz and suggested that I be made a rear admiral on his staff, and gave the reasons why it would facilitate my doing my job, and then after he sent the letter he showed it to me. I told him I didn't think I should be, and being a rear admiral wouldn't make a bit of difference in the way I was running that job, and I don't think it would have. And I told him why and a asked him if he had any objections if I were to go see Admiral Nimitz and explain to him, next time I went back to Pearl, why I shouldn't be. He said no. So next time I went back I did see Admiral Nimitz and told him why, and he never put it in, and I think rightly so, because you get out of step, too far out of step--it's all right to go a little bit further, but if you get too far out of step, you're overcoming too many obstacles, there's too much experience you do not have, so much you don't understand. But worse than that is if you get people in high places too soon, they've got to get out of high places too soon, so it's very costly and expensive to the service to have too young people in it, because of retirement pay. For example, even though I served six years as CNO, I still got out, there was no place for me to go--I retired when I was 59, and at that time, I was a better officer than I'd ever been before.

Q: You were at the peak of your . . .

Burke: . . . yes, and it would have been good if the Navy could have used that, used me for a couple of more years. It would have saved that much retirement pay, saved that many officers; and as it was, why, I went out, and the Navy lost that service. Now, of course, that's a question of opinion as to whether or not I was worth it or not, but still that's generally true.

Q: At one point the Navy had the mechanism for using such talent in the General Board, whether it was used effectively or not is another question, but that was the intent, was it not?

Burke: Yes, it was. I was on the General Board once as a captain, and it was a good board. It was a good idea. But it did require the General Board addressing the proper problems, which they frequently did not. They were told to study some problem which was not a very important one. It also required quicker action that the General Board usually took, and it also required the officials, the management (since this was an advisory board) of the Navy pay some attention to it. Otherwise the General Board members said, "To hell with this, we're just marking time and there's no reason for it." And they themselves didn't do a very good job.

Q: There were flaws in that system.

Burke: There are great flaws in the system but they can be overcome. We tried to overcome it. The reason why we were put on the General Board, there were three or four captains and colonels--surprisingly enough, Colonel Pate who later became Commandant of the Marine Corps, Saavy Hoffman of '22, and I and one other captain at some later time, were assigned to the General Board to do the legwork and also to see if we could put some life into it.

Q: Vitalize it.

Burke: Vitalize it. Now, the head of the General Board initially was Admiral Towers. He was a good man. And Admiral Sock McMorris, who died later, (both of them dead by now), succeeded him. Both of them were very good people, and they worked hard. I think they accomplished something.

Q: But it really needed that mixture of more youthful people on the Board.

Burke: It did--it needed a little stirring up. Not so much youthful as it was stirring up, somebody to bring in some problems, which we didn't bring in, but to go out and find out what you thought were the most important problems, and to get the CNO's office to send those problems down for study.

Q: Sort of keep the Board with it until they came up with some suggestions. You said earlier that you felt that you were too young to be CNO. Would you or do you advocate a sort of system of understudy to the CNO to step in eventually?

Burke: Well, theoretically I do, and I did advocate that while I was still on active duty, but my civilian life has led me to doubt that that ever really worked as well as it might work. It ought to, but it doesn't. There are very few civilian organizations that have an understudy for their chief executive officer. They have--and usually when they do, that understudy doesn't turn out. I mean, sometimes when they do the understudy doesn't turn out to be a good man, a good chief executive officer himself. Now, instead of that, what should happen I think is to have several people, all of whom are qualified to become chief executive officer, in a company, or in a military organization and then, if one of them doesn't--you've got competition for the job in an indirect sort of way, so they work harder for it. They try to fit themselves for the job. Also you have alternatives, and you still have those alternatives after one man is appointed, and if he fails.

Now, several times in civilian life, the chief executive officer of some company of which I've been a director has not done as well as he should. Then you have to fire him, get rid of him and get a new chief executive officer, and it's very horrible to do that, because the board picked the first one in the first place and has made a mistake. But you can never tell what a man will do until he gets the buck on his shoulder. He gets that full authority and full responsibility, and then some of them buckle under the tremendous load. Some of them become arrogant and feel that they themselves--they confuse themselves with their company, and they feel that they have a lot more authority than they actually have. And sometimes they just simply are not able to run the business. They don't know enough or they don't make proper decisions.

The same is true in the Navy. When I was--I put in my request for retirement before the election of 1960 so there would be no political implications. I wanted to retire. Six years is long enough--both for the good of the Navy and for myself. And so I wanted to, I submitted my resignation, to be held until the new administration came in. President Eisenhower accepted it, and then as soon as President Kennedy came in he wanted me to stay on for a while, and I said no, I've submitted this resignation, it's all set, I have no implications whatever except that it's bad for one man to stay at the head of the service too long, and it's bad for me, I'm running down.

So they asked me--Franke was Secretary of the Navy but Gates was Secretary of Defense--and so Gates said, "Give me a list of people who can relieve you."

Well, I spent several weeks on that list, and I went down every flag officer list, and when I ended up I had about 40 people on the list, 40 people that I thought were qualified, some better than others.

Q: That certainly speaks well for the Navy.

Burke: Yes, it did. There are a lot of very good people, and this depended on what kind of man they wanted, what they wanted him to do, and so forth . . . They weren't all equally good.

They said, "This is no good, you've got to cut it down." Too much of a problem. "You give me the name of the man that you would have become--the best man."

I said, "No, I won't do this, and the reason I won't do it is because, I won't do it unless you guarantee to appoint him. If he will be appointed and you guarantee it, I'll do it, but otherwise I won't, and the reason why is that if I think a man is best and recommend him to you and he is not appointed, there will be a leak. Somehow there will be a leak. And that man will be ruined. He will know he was not selected, that he was offered up and he was not selected, and it would be very bad for him. On the other hand, if he were selected, it might be just about as bad because he would be known as Burke's boy. So the same old policies, and you wouldn't be free for independent action."

Well, they kept working on me so eventually I said, "I'll give you six names," and I worked it down to six, and they were six damn good officers. Any one of them could have been CNO and would have made a good one. I never wrote that list down, never typed it. It was a verbal thing. Even then, there are people who made some very astute guesses as to who those six were. In other words, there were leaks.

Q: Well, you've been in public life long enough to know that there are leaks.

Burke: There are leaks. One of them was selected. Anderson was on my list. He was one of them, yes.

Q: As you were talking I thought of a reverse side of the coin. Inasmuch as you were named CNO when you were relatively young, this enabled you to serve a longer period of time than would have been the lot of most men. I think you served longer than anyone else.

Burke: Yes, but I could have served--in the first place, staying too long in the head job, in civilian life eight years is about long enough. Eight years is really--and a service chief has more strain than a chief executive in a civilian company. But if it had just come later, I could have served until I was 62 well enough, and as it was the Navy lost a couple of years. I should still have been appointed later.

Q: Well, sir, shall we go back now to your initial appointment in the year 1955. You came into office in August, succeeding Admiral Carney.

Burke: Yes. I was appointed--I heard about it in probably May. I had gone to see the President several times. Admiral Carney sent me over to the Far East to make a tour there, and then I had to study my lesson, all the problems, so I think I started that tour--I think I came down to Washington probably in June, and spent the latter part of June and July preparing. At the end of July, I remember they had a conference of the Defense Department down at Quantico, and I went down there for that conference--flag officers of all the services. I came in on the 15th of August succeeding

Admiral Carney.

Q: The Far East was certainly the hot spot that year in terms of international relations.

Burke: That is right. As a matter of fact, this was one of the things that caused a great deal of difficulty in the Department of Defense. Some of the military people thought that war would break out and there would be fighting in the Far East, and they wanted to be prepared for it, and some of them made predictions that didn't turn out, but they were based upon reasonable assumptions.

Q: During your tour of the Far East, did you look in on the SEATO powers?

Burke: No, I went primarily to the--to Southeast Asia. I went to Japan, Taiwan, Korea, I think. I went to Thailand, Cambodia, Laos, and Vietnam. Philippines. I think that was all.

Q: And visited the Seventh Fleet, no doubt?

Burke: Visited the Seventh Fleet, yes.

Q: Did you have any specific mission in mind when you went or was it just fact gathering?

Burke 1 - 18

Burke: No. Well, it was just a learning period, for me to meet the people in those nations, to meet the Navy operating people and other service people in the area, and to acquaint myself with what was happening in the area, as that was the hot area.

Q: Your knowledge of that area was fairly extensive to begin with, wasn't it?

Burke: Yes, but a year makes a lot a difference. I'd spent a year or so in the Atlantic.

Q: Do you recall how you were received in various places? How you were received in Japan, where we had signed a Mutual Defense Treaty with them the previous year?

Burke: Very well. Remember I was a two star Admiral then. I was a rear admiral, and when I made this tour, I remember I got a shock when I went to the first place, when I got four star honors. But people were very good. There wasn't a single occasion where I wasn't given all the information I wanted, where they didn't seem to be happy to see me and wanting to help. They were always good. This was particularly true in Japan and Korea and Taiwan where I had a lot of friends.

Q: What about Saigon? This was the year following the

the French defeat.

Burke: They were very concerned. I've forgotten who--Diem was in Vietnam, yes, and I had great admiration for him. I thought he was very good. I remember being put up in his guest house and talking with him at some length. He was very good at explaining things, very intense man, and I liked him very much. I liked the Prime Minister of Thailand too.

Q: Sarit?

Burke: Right. He was good.

Q: He was a military man, was he not?

Burke: Yes. Both of them were.

Q: Did Admiral Stump accompany you?

Burke: No. No, because he had a big job to do other than hold my hand, but Admiral Stump was an example of what--see, when I became Chief of Naval Operations, one of the conditions under which I took the job, (and I had several conditions,) one of them was that because I had such great admiration for a lot of my seniors, that I was not going to clean house. I was not going to fire a lot of people who were my seniors. Well, I had been with Admiral Stump during the war. He was a very good fighting man. He had some spots that I didn't like, of course, just as I had spots that he didn't like. He's a tough man. But he was a very fine man, and I have never had anybody that helped me as much as he tried to do when he was CINCPAC and I was CNO. He did everything he could to make things run the way I wanted them run. And I had to lean over backwards to make sure that I didn't suggest something that I didn't intent to suggest, because he'd try to do it. It was remarkable what those senior people did. Admiral Wright was the same way. But Felix Stump was one of the finest people I've ever known for his support. He was good.

Of course, I got my best information from him and from his staff at Pearl.

Q: You were briefed on the way out.

Burke: And briefed on the way back.

Q: He had a very efficient staff.

Burke: He did have, he had a good staff.

Q: Well, when you came back and as you assumed the job, did you have a conference with the President?

Burke: Well, I had several conferences with the President

before I went.

Q: Did he have any specific instructions?

Burke: Oh yes. His big one was, how did I work for the other services? How much did I know of the other services? And he insisted, I guess he told me half a dozen times in two of three meetings that my big job was not to head the Navy, my big job was my job as a member of the Joint Chiefs of Staff, that the Joint Chiefs of Staff position was the most important position.

I tried to explain to him that I thought that the reason I would make a good member of the Joint Chiefs of Staff, if I did, was because I knew the Navy and I was to present the Navy point of view, or a point of view because of my experience in the Navy.

Well, he agreed with that, but he also felt that being a member of the Joint Chiefs of Staff was most important, as it was.

Q: He preferred the greater emphasis on the unity of the services.

Burke: And I preferred, I believed then and believe now that it's not so important to have unity; what is important is to make sure that all the facts and all the factors pertaining to the problem are each brought out very clearly and then if there are differences of opinion, the President has to make a decision. Now, this President Eisenhower did not want to do. He didn't want these problems coming up to him, he wanted them settled down below, and it was one of the things that we had difficulty--he had difficulty with me the whole time, and with the other Chiefs too. Naturally a man who's brought up in the Air Force, if he's a good Air Force officer, (and they are or they wouldn't be chief of their service), he believes in what the Air Force can do. He believes the Air Force is the best damned service in the whole world, and when he sees a job, when he sees something needs to be done, he thinks of how can the Air Force do it? And the same is true with the Army and Navy.

Well, naturally conflicts develop. Now, if those conflicts are clearly brought out and the points are clearly understood, and that's not too difficult, then somebody can make--above all the services, which is the President--can make a decision and it's not too difficult.

Q: I would imagine, a certain percentage of the time, the Joint Chiefs themselves can make a decision based on all the facts.

Burke: The Joint Chiefs can make a decision based on all the facts, so long as it doesn't involve an allocation of money to the services, or missions of the services. Now, you can resolve everything but the interfaces and missions. But you cannot resolve--the Chiefs cannot resolve the money problem, and there is no militaryman that can. Unless he is appointed above all other military . . . . Then he can. And if he does, he's very apt to--not to weigh the factors that are brought before him equitably. In a place like Spain, for example, where they have a single chief of staff, Franco was the chief of staff, his own chief of staff, and it's an army, it's a land concept--their security is based upon their land ability--that's quite all right. But in a nation like the United States or England or even Russia, they suffer from ignorance of the top man--this is what happened in the USSR for years--the top people were Army oriented, and they never understood a navy until the Cuban missile crisis. They never really understood it.

Q: That's obvious based on the facts.

Burke: Yes. Well, they studied like hell right after World War II--they put a tremendous amount of study, both on materielle, for example, in missiles they got all the German scientists and things like that, they got as much knowledge as they could. They also did a lot of theoretical studies on logistics--how was it, why was it that the Allies won? What factors were there? What factors were there in Germany losing when she had so much capability? Things must have been done differently. And they came to the conclusion in those studies, even then--they didn't ever release the studies but it was evident--that they realized that seapower was a very important factor. But seapower up until that time, as far as Russia had been concerned, was always tied to the flanks of the Army. Even Rojectvensky in the Battle of Tsushima, where he lost the Battle of Tsushima so horribly--even then, he did that. That was caused primarily because the Navy had never operated as a high seas fleet.

The Soviets understood this all right, that a big nation that was dependent upon the sea had to have sea power to protect the sea, protect its own communications. They realized, too, that the Soviet Union was not so dependent on the sea as the United States or most of the other nations because she had a lot of material, but still if she wanted to whip us she had to have some way of driving us off the sea, of wresting control away from us, of preventing us from having it. But it was a theoretical study. They didn't know what to do about it, and they didn't really realize the significance of it until in the Cuban missile crisis, they were suddenly confronted with the fact. They couldn't move. They couldn't move. And so at that time, they went to work so that the next time they could move. That was the watershed. Up until that time it had been theoretical discussion. Then they started to go to work, and this is when they started pushing their Navy out to the high seas, developing equipment which they could use to destroy our Navy, and seize control of the seas themselves, but mostly to prevent us from having control of the seas, and they've done a good job.

Q: Admiral going back to the Joint Chiefs, can the chairman of the Joint Chiefs, although he comes from one of the services, can he rise above that individual service in his capacity as chairman? Was Admiral Radford able to do this?

Burke: No. No. You talk about rising above--Admiral Radford--because he wanted to do this, he did not want to be a naval officer and stay with the Navy, so he was very careful always, if there was any doubt, the Navy lost. He was my hardest antagonist, because he was a naval officer, he knew a lot about the Navy, he thought that he knew more about it than I did--well, he might have, I don't know-- but he would give a decision to the Air Froce and the Army rather than the Navy when it was an even break, because he did not ever want to be accused, or did not ever want to be, in a position of favoring the Navy. So he leaned over backwards. Now, Twining did the same way but to a lesser extent.

Q: Did the Navy fare better under those circumstances?

Burke: Yes. I could persuade Twining easier than I could Radford. And Radford's a hell of a good friend of mine. He's a fine fellow, but that was a bad characteristic. Twining was a wonderful man, too.

Now, the Army people are not so much that way. Lemnitzer was pretty much. He was a good man. But you take my friend Collins--he could never rise above his service. Bradley couldn't. Omar Bradley--I had quite a bit to do with him, but I don't think, in spite of the fact that I liked Bradley as a man and he was a very good Army officer, he nearly always favored the Army. Taylor nearly always favored the Army.

Q: What about General Eisenhower himself, when he was forced to a decision on things that hadn't been decided in a Joint Chiefs? Was he able to be Commander-in-Chief of all the services?

Burke: Yes. Yes, he had had so much difficulty with de Gaulle and some of the other supporting commanders during the war that he could make decisions pretty objectively, for the good of the country. He really tried. Sometimes it was hard to convince him of capabilities. But he made just decisions on what he believed. He didn't consciously ever favor the Army. As a matter of fact, he was a little bit like Radford. He gave the Army a bad time sometimes, because he knew the Army's weaknesses.

Q: Could you give me an illustration of his impartiality?

Burke: Yes. Well, he wanted to withdraw troops from Europe and he wanted to cut down the European Army force a lot more than the Army wanted, and I think even more than we wanted to at that time, the rest of the Chiefs, at that time.

Q: This is a little later on.

Burke: Yes. But because he knew the weaknesses and the strengths he could make as good a judgment on the psychological effects of reducing Army forces as we could. There are differences of opinion on that, but he could very easily have favored the Army, as Taylor did later when he was Chairman. But as far as the Navy was concerned, he went to sea on carriers when he was President. We tried to give him as much instruction as possible. But he never really understood the full extent of it. But he listened, and he made decisions that I could go fight for carriers. He didn't tell me no. He didn't encourage me much sometimes.

Q: Add another one to the . . .

Burke: Yes. Yes. You know, I think President Eisenhower always tried to do what he thought was best for his country, no matter what, and I think he tried to analyze it carefully. He wasn't always right, but he tried. So did Truman.

Q: I imagine the Navy seized every opportunity for indoctrination of the President--his trips abroad, his trips to Bermuda to the various conferences he attended, he went by boat, did he not?

Burke: Yes. We tried to arrange that.

Q: Through his naval aide?

Burke: Through his naval aide. Sometimes with the President himself. See, I had a big argument with the President-- not argument, I had a very unfortunate experience when I first became CNO. At that time, we were short of people.

The Navy was very short of people and we were laying up ships, and it was a question of whether we lay up more ships and take a much reduced number of personnel, or go to the draft, and they had made the decision, the Secretary of Navy, Secretary of Defense and the President had agreed, upon advice of Admiral Carney too (whom I greatly admire also) had agreed that the Navy would not go to the draft but instead would remain a volunteer service and would reduce its number of ships to fit whatever it could get as volunteers. They expected that the volunteers would level off at a rather high position and we would not have any great difficulty in manning most of our ships.

Well, I had studied that damn problem backwards and forwards. It was one of the worst ones that I was confronted with. The decision had been made, but I wasn't so sure that we wouldn't have to go to the draft.

Well, in the time between--I don't know exactly when the President made that decision, but probably June when he made that, maybe earlier . . .

Q: Of '55?

Burke: Of '55--and our Navy kept going down . . . . Situation got worse. And by the time I took over, I thought we were in a very bad way, and I talked with Admiral Holloway, who was Chief of Bupers then, as to what he thought the answers were. Bupers felt that we should go to the draft, but not very strongly, although Admiral Holloway himself felt rather strongly about it.

Well, I was convinced after listening to their reasons and their analysis of the problem that we would have to go to the draft. So I went up to see the Secretary of the Navy and told him that I thought we had to go to the draft, and he said, "No, we've settled that question. This has been a very serious thing and we've worked on it, we've studied it, and we have decided not to go to the draft."

I said, "Well, I think it's wrong, I think we should go to the draft."

He said, "Your predecessor agreed that we should not go to the draft, that we should have a volunteer Navy."

I said, "This situation's a little bit different now."

He said, "No, it hasn't become much different. Now, you just go back and work on those problems you can do something about. Don't worry about this one, this decision's been made."

So I did. I went back for a couple of days. It didn't get any better. I thought it over and I asked for some more data, all the data I could get, and I came to the conclusion, we've got to go to the draft.

So I went back to Mr. Thomas, and he was still insistent that we not go to the draft. I said, "Mr. Secretary, then I must see the President."

He said, "You can't do that."

I said, "It says in the law that I--that any time I want to, I can see the President. And this is something that I think is serious enough so that the President should know, and I think what's being done is wrong."

So he said, "Well, let's go down and see Charlie Wilson." So I went down to see Mr. Wilson and explained to him, with Mr. Thomas, and Mr. Wilson tried to dissuade me and I said, "No, I want to see the President."

So we called up and made an appointment to see the President that afternoon, and Mr. Wilson took us over to the White House in his car. This was maybe with a week after I'd become CNO.

Q: That was a very courageous step on your part.

Burke: No, it wasn't courageous. It was something that needed to be done. I went over there, and, of course, we got over there a little early, and I walked up and down the outer office for 15 or 20 minutes that we were waiting, and I thought, "Who am I? The President has made the decision and the Secretary of Defense, the Secretary of the Navy, they all think the decision is right, and who am I to pit my knowledge, which is incomplete, and I've just found out I don't know very much, against that, against their knowledge and be so damn stubborn? Maybe I'm wrong, and I shouldn't have done this."

I seriously thought maybe I ought to go tell them, forget it. Then I realized, I'd brought up the subject, I'd taken a stand, and if I back down now, I've had it. I will never again be able to make a decision. And damn it, I really am right. What worries me is not the fact that I think I'm wrong, but the fact that I might be wrong and that I'm scared of bucking the organization."

So I went in to see the President, and they asked me to explain my position courteously to the President first, and I did. Then Mr. Thomas and Mr. Wilson explained their position, why they thought I was wrong.

Eisenhower understood exactly what position I'd put him in. We discussed the thing a little bit more. He understood all about the draft, too. He said, "Well, we can go to the draft. We'll go to the draft."

Q: He made his decision then.

Burke: Yes, right then. He had to. I put him in a spot

where he had to fire me right then, or he had to do what I asked him to do. Now, it's not quite that, but nearly that.

Q: The lines were clearly drawn.

Burke: They were clearly drawn. And if he fired me, there would have been all hell break lose. They'd just gone through the turmoil of dipping deep for me, and if they fired me in a week or so, it would have been a hell of a thing. And he couldn't do it. He also, I think, realized that I was right. But the Navy was very proud of being a volunteer service, and we have probably leaned over too far to keep it that way and been hurt in the process.

Well, anyway, I put him in a terrible spot, because he had to change a decision that had been made and he had to go against the Secretary of Defense and Secretary of the Navy.

Q: Both of whom were basically civilians, however.

Burke: Both of whom were civilians. Both of whom were good men, though. I remember it very well because the President asked me to stay in just a minute after the other two left, and I've forgotten what he told me but I got the import all right. I've forgotten the words but I got the import: "Young man, you put me in a hell of a spot." And he didn't like it at all. He was furious. I had forced him into a position which he didn't like.

Well, when I went out, Mr. Wilson and Mr. Thomas had gone, to hell with me, they left me over there without a car. So I had to call up and get a car and go back to the Pentagon. Mr. Thomas and Mr. Wilson, Mr. Thomas particularly was very distant and very official and very cold. He thought he had probably made a big mistake in recommending me in the first place. Not impolite, not rough or anything like that, but he didn't like what I had done.

Well, the nice part about that was, it came about although I didn't know what I was doing. I had been picked very low. I'd been selected, deep selection, and I was supposed to be, indicated that I was the Secretary's man-- I was Thomas's boy and Mr. Wilson's boy. And this indicated to the Navy and to the President that I was not. I was independent, and probably a wrong and stubborn bastard, which I had warned them about in the first place.

So later on, after I'd gotten to know the President, he sometimes sent for me on problems that had nothing to do whatever with the Navy. Sometimes not even with the military. And usually about 5 o'clock in the afternoon, just before dinner, sometimes 6 o'clock--I'd come over. I liked old fashioneds, he liked old fashioneds, and we'd have a drink, and he would bring up the problems he wanted to discuss. First they were all connected with the military, sometimes not Navy. When they were not Navy problems I'd say, "Mr. President, I'm not familiar with all the details of this."

He said, "I don't want you to be. I want to get an off the top of your head opinion."

And I would give it to him as well as I knew how. Mostly I never knew what decision he finally took. But the nice part about that was that after a little while, I realized that what he was doing, he could trust my statements insofar as they were the best I could give him.

Q: This was integrity he saw . . .

Burke: I don't know what--yes, some of it was integrity, but he had somebody to talk to, to play things against, and he needed that, somebody who had some knowledge of some of the things. Now, a President needs that very much. I wasn't the only one that he did that with by any means. But this is one of the things that's needed, is somebody to give you their opinion, even though it's not an expert opinion, based upon a general observation; what's good for the country is very hard to find out, very hard to determine, and you have to make sure you're not letting some personal prejudice ride in it.

Q: Especially when you're in the White House, surrounded by . . .

Burke: Yes . . .

Q: . . . a protective force . . . .

Burke: President Eisenhower recognized that. And because he did, he was a very fine President. He was not a brilliant man, and he'd get mad as hell sometimes. He'd get awfully furious. He'd forget it pretty soon too, when he got mad. But his decisions were based upon what he thought was good for the United States, I think always, not on what was good for Eisenhower.

Q: Going back to that incident again, how long did it take to establish better relationships with Secretary Thomas?

Burke: Oh, maybe a couple of weeks. He's a wonderful little man. He's a very fine man. I had a lot of trouble with Mr. Thomas. We had lots of differences of opinion. But we're very good friends now. He's one of the best friends I have, I think. But we had trouble particularly--when he would like to see, he wanted to see me move fast in replacing some of the older officers, and I had had that as a condition on which I took office. Some of them, I would have removed sooner if he hadn't tried to force me. But when he would get on a particular man and say, "You've got to get rid of him," I'd say, "no." So I'd hang on too long, longer than I really should have, because I wouldn't-- didn't want to be pressured into doing something.

Q: He came to see the merit of your ability to stand on your hind legs, too?

Burke: I don't know. I'm not sure that was a correct analysis of it. I never could quite reach the point where I could accept something--I never accepted it quite soon enough, sometimes. The things that I eventually had to give on, and did give on, I could have given on a little sooner. But it's just like the Stock Market or anything else, you never hit the high point or the low point, hit it exactly right.

Q: Admiral, at the very beginning of 1956, Secretary Dulles wrote an article for LIFE MAGAZINE in which he, I think, first proclaimed what later was termed his policy of 'brinkmanship.' Can you talk about that and its relation to the Navy and its policy?

Burke: Well, yes. Dulles was a man that I also greatly admired. I guess it was during the Quemoy-Matsu affair, or maybe it was when a plane was shot down, one of our planes was shot down. In any case, I went over to see Mr. Dulles at his house on a Sunday afternoon, or Sunday morning. He had a little study and a little round table there, and we discussed the problem that I'd brought up, and he had five piles of papers on the little table. When I was about to leave, I said, "Mr. Secretary, what the hell are those five piles for?"

He said, "Well, these are the things I've got to do-- this is the UN, this is a draft memorandum I've got to draw up, this is something else."

"Why don't you get somebody on your staff to do that?"

He said, "Because they will put their own ideas in it, and it's much more difficult for me to correct a paper that's already been written than it is to write it in the first place."

I said, "You'll never finish it, let me help you-- on what?"

"Take this one," and it was a memorandum to the UN. So I wrote an outline of what I thought should be the memorandum. That helped him. So I used to go over and see him, not frequently but every once in a while, and discuss naval power, the use of power, national power in foreign nations to influence the trend of events which every nation wanted to do. Secretary Dulles--his policy was named 'brinkmanship', (he may have named it himself,) but it wasn't really that. It was a use of power or the possible use of power to influence other nations to come his way. And this was what--on this brinkmanship business, on this massive retaliation, this was to --he knew very well that you could not, that the United States could not force its way on all other nations simply by using atomic weapons. It needed a lot more than that. And in that same speech or article he also made a statement that the punishment should fit the crime. But what he did want to do was for the United States to have all the elements of national power in its grasp, and to use them cleverly without dissipation of that power, and still not try to gain an objective which was not compatible with long range United States interest, which is humanity. The people all over, stability in the world.

He was quite willing, quite willing to--he understood very well the little uses of power, the use of economic and political means, psychological means as well as military means, to gain--to keep from being taken.

What he understood was that a nation must be willing to use power in order to have that power become credible, and a willingness to use power means that sometimes nations won't believe you're going to use it just by taking a stance. You have to actually use it. So you can't threaten idly the use of power, unless it's a situation where you really should use power if it becomes necessary.

Now, one of the circumstances that Mr. Dulles--that I was very much impressed with Mr. Dulles was, you remember, (I've forgotten the date but I think about 1957,) we had a seaplane, reconnaissance plane shot down off the China coast. This plane was based in Japan, and flew a reconnaissance flight down the China coast, out at sea more than 12 miles, and it was shot down. We knew approximately where it was shot down, and we got word very quickly, that it was shot down, so I ordered the Seventh Fleet--I don't know where it was but I think it was around Okinawa, but I ordered the Seventh Fleet down to search for this plane just beyond the three mile limit, being very careful not to violate the three mile limit, but also being very careful that we did not extend that search to a place where it was not obvious that we were going outside the three miles. This was the use both of aircraft and of ships, so we stayed right on the three mile line, being careful not to get inside, but also just as close as they could be and still be sure they were not . . .

Q: A razor's edge.

Burke: A razor's edge, and also for the planes to fly that way.

Well, of course, as soon as I issued those orders--in those days I had command of the fleets, CNO did--as soon as I issued those orders, which I issued in my own right, I went over to see Mr. Dulles, right quick. I notified the Joint Chiefs but I went over to see Mr. Dulles right quick and he said, "My God, don't do that!"

I said, "Mr. Dulles, it's very important--the Chinese shot down one of our airplanes, and we're going to do everything that's permitted in international law to get it back. We're going to search for that, we're going to search--it may have gone down in international waters, it might have, and we've got to do that."

He said, "There must be some other way, why don't you put them out a little bit further?"

I said, "No, it's got to be three miles." There's a difference between three miles and 12 miles. I said, "If we put them at 12 miles, (we don't recognize 12 miles, we recognize three miles)--the Chinese say 12 miles, OK, we say three miles. That's what we recognize. That's we've stated in all our public statements, so damn it, we've got to put the Fleet on three miles and we've got to really search."

He said, "That's a question for the President to decide."

I said, "That's right," so we went over to see the President, and the President also brought up the same thing that Mr. Dulles did, "Why can't you do it a little easier?" But he saw it, and Mr. Dulles saw it, too. Mr. Dulles wouldn't recommend that but he was perfectly willing to accept it. So he said, all right . . . So we searched. We never found the plane. We searched for a week or so, and obviously, if you don't find the plane within that time, you're not going to find the plane.

Then Mr. Dulles said, "Why don't you withdraw the Fleet now?"

I said, "No, sir. Let's stay there so that we rub it in just a little bit. We make sure that they recognize that we're mad."

So he agreed. Now, that's the use of power. Never again did they shoot down one of our planes. That's the use of power. It doesn't do anything--the plane actually was shot down and sank some place, nobody knew what happened. But they understood that.

Again, in Quemoy and Matsu, when the Red Chinese decided they were going to try to take Quemoy and Matsu, we were in force in Taiwan, and they reinforced both those islands. Then it looked like they were going to launch-- they launched heavy artillery attacks against these islands, and they were destroying a lot. And they needed to be re-supplied, the logistics were getting bad, and these artillery attacks could probably sink ships.

So how do you stop that? How do the Nationalist Chinese supply those outpost garrisons? Well, they knew a little bit about amphibious warfare but they didn't know very much, and I wanted to put in our own amphibious force of logistics, just to get supplies to Quemoy and Matsu.

That's international relations. The President said, "No, we can't do that." I said, "Can we train them?" He said, "Sure."

So we gave them lots of training and we gave them lots of LSDs and ships, boats, to supply the thing, and it wasn't a question of immediate attack, it was a question of wearing them down and eventually attacking.

So at that time, I said, "We will escort these ships in international waters, is that all right, Mr. President?"

"Yes, all right, go ahead."

"What's international waters?"

I said, "Three miles." He said, "Oh, no you don't, we have run through that, we can't do that. You keep those ships 12 miles out."

I said, "I'd like to put them in at three miles."

He said, "No, you keep them 12 miles out. This is a different problem," and I agreed that it was, "from the problem before."

I said, "All right, I'm grateful for that." So we did and the Chinese reinforced their garrisons and put their supplies in caves.

Well, the question was, why the hell do you need Quemoy and Matsu? They're little bits of islands, they're outposts, but they're symbolic. They were symbolic. As I told Mr. Eisenhower then, "They don't mean anything, it's a purely symbolic thing, they don't mean anything except, who's daddy? Who runs that part of the world, the Red Chinese or the Nationalist Chinese? But physically it doesn't make any difference." I said, "It's just like the virtue of a man's wife. The wife is the same. But you don't let anybody else attack her. You just don't do it. These are Nationalist Chinese islands, and they have to be held, or they have to be abandoned voluntarily before they're threatened, before they're made to abandon them."

Now, Dulles understood that very well, and he supported

that wholeheartedly, and so did the President. No difficulty.

Dulles also knew the timing of things was very important. In Lebanon, I had sent the Sixth Fleet to sea a great many times in the expectation that something would happen in Lebanon. It never happened. But still you have to be ready. The President was asking me how long--when this thing, the Lebanon affair finally got bad again--he asked me how long, how much warning I needed for a landing. I told him, "Twenty-four hours."

This is when we had three battalions in the Mediterranean and the Sixth Fleet was at sea, I'd ordered it to sea. Well, President Eisenhower knew--he knew distances, he knew timing, how important it is for events to occur at exactly the right time sometimes. And I knew he did, and I had a general idea that what he was planning on doing was to land at the last possible time that would be effective for President Chamoun.

The time that would be most effective for him, and as late as possible so that we wouldn't take any steps that would be unnecessary.

So as time went on I kept moving the fleet, advising Admiral Holloway who had the CincNelm command and Admiral Cat Brown who had the Sixth Fleet, to move closer to Lebanon, all set for a landing.

They finally gave us thirtten hours, I think, rather than twenty-four. Fortunately, I had fudged on it a little too, and they could land exactly 3 o'clock in the afternoon, which they did.

Now, they understood that. That was a good operation from their point of view. They did some good things. The timing was good. The execution was good, too.

Now in the Suez crisis, that was not--Mr. Dulles was so damned angry at the Egyptians and also the Russians, and also the British and the French, that he did not want to help. He wanted to remain absolutely neutral. He didn't want to help the British and French. And the British, for the first time in a long, long time, gave orders when they were unprepared to execute them, and, of course, the Suez landing was a fiasco. At that time I wanted to help the British, even giving them some of our amphibious force over there, but they (our officials) said no. I think that was a mistake. I think it would have been good had we persuaded the British to be sure that they would be successful in their landing and then to help them be successful.

One of the things that's very important is, when you start an operation like that you've got to be willing to carry it all the way through real hard, and be pretty sure you've got the capability of doing it. This is what we did not do in the Vietnam War, among other things.

Q: The psychological impact on Britain itself was very great, since she couldn't carry on.

Burke: She couldn't carry on. Mountbatten came over here right after that, and he said that he had briefed the Cabinet . . .

Q: . . . Eden was Prime Minister . . . .

Burke: Yes, Eden was Prime Minister. Mountbatten briefed the Cabinet on what was required for Britain to operate, (and they had quite a bit of material in Malta, mostly small landing ships) and he gave them a time of preparation which I think was a week and said, "If you give us a week, then a week later we will sail from Malta," and then he gave a schedule of what they could do.

Well, they didn't pay any attention to that schedule, the Cabinet didn't. When the Prime Minister gave orders to the British forces, they didn't give them the time that was necessary to carry out those orders. So they had to sail over with too few people and operate without a good plan, whereas the initial schedule had been all right.

Q: Why weren't we in on the planning?

Burke: It happens all the time—people get mad. Nations are like children, unfortunately. They're people. A nation feels that Nation A has not informed Nation B soon enough of something, or has done something to Nation B, so Nation B wants to take action and it doesn't want to tell Nation A. It doesn't. So pretty soon it gets so that there's very little communication, and they don't really inform each other. Sometimes for good reason one nation will let the information out of the bag or will cross you up or something like that. But lots of times it's just pique.

This is what's the matter with Japan right now. Japan is very picqued. I've had Japanese in here—Mr. Oi represents a flock of Japanese newspapers, and he's picqued.

Q: Because of the President's action in going to Peking?

Burke: Yes, he says the Nixon shocks, the two Nixon shocks. This man writes for the (Japanese newspaper) SHIMBUN. But he brings up all the things that the United States has done, and he ignores the things that Japan has done in retaliation. This is natural. This has happened over and over again.

Q: Pride is involved.

Burke: Pride is involved, you didn't tell it, and so "we're

going to hurt you a little bit," an eye for an eye, and it's not such a bad policy, but you've got to recognize that it exists.

Q: I often wondered in the case of the Suez crisis if a failure to acquaint the United States with the contemplated move on the part of Britain and France was not influenced in part by France and her sensitivity, which greater than the British.

Burke: Sure, I'm sure it was. I'm sure it was, but also the British. They didn't want to be beholden to Uncle Sam.

Q: Admiral, to go back to something you mentioned just in passing, that was the Eisenhower-Dulles doctrine of massive retaliation. Inasmuch as you were an integral part of the administration, do you really believe that if forced to the wall we would have used our power?

Burke: Yes. I think we would have. Now, not on little things. You can't use a sledgehammer to kill a fly. Nor should you use unnecessary force to accomplish a thing, but you've got to use enough force to make sure you accomplish your task that you set out to do.

So if Germany, if Russia invaded Germany, for example,

Burke 1 - 50

we would have launched, I think. Probably we would have launched. If the President thought that Russia had attacked one of our allies, one of the NATO allies or attacked the NATO nations, I think he would have launched. Now, I don't know that. I think it. It's a hell of a decision on the President, too, but I think that's what held the Soviets off, because it would be very easy for the Soviets to ttake the next step and say, this is such a horrible decision for the U. S. to make that we can attack, we can take quite a bit of territory without danger of being attacked, and they won't be able to do anything about it because they'll (the U.S.) be afraid of world opinion, afraid of making that God awful decision of launching atomic weapons.

So this is what they might do now--that and the fact that they have atomic retaliation power now, too.

Q: One other aspect of that doctrine has always intrigued me. I wonder if the fact that it was proclaimed, and the populace of the United States bought it, if there didn't develop as a result among our people a certain sense of complacency about conventional warfare, and conventional weapons?

Burke: Well, yes, this is true, and the Air Force sponsored that a good deal. They supported that view, that all you need is air power and all you need is atomic weapons. Now, not everybody in the Air Force, but generally speaking, Air Force people. This is not true. The President and Mr. Dulles certainly knew that you have to have all kinds--you had to have all kinds of military forces and they had to be properly balanced. There's no one outfit can do it all by itself. There was no one reliance, no one thing that you could rely on. You've got to have the full capability, from the most minute action up to the greatest, and you've got to be able to defeat an enemy ship for ship, company for company or airplane by airplane, all the way up the line, and you've got to be able to win the war. Or if you can't do that, if you're so small and incapable of winning the war, the enemy has to be convinced that you have enough capability and that you're willing to use that capability so that you will make it unprofitable for him to attack. This is the value of Switzerland's neutrality. This is what Sweden's military is trying to do and Swedish civilian people of course, civilian government, think is unnecessary.

But I think Truman, Eisenhower both understood that very well. Now, Eisenhower did develop, permitted or encouraged us to develop weapons systems for conventional forces. Sometimes he'd get Air Force opposition but still it was done.

Q: The overall understanding was not as clear, I believe, when one reads the press and thinks of one's experiences living through those years. I don't think the people understood too well because the emphasis was always on saving money and cutting down on the budget and balancing the budget.

Burke: Well, that's right. But it was there. We did not ever achieve a real excellent military posture. We had a good one but not a real excellent one. I don't suppose any nation ever does, unless they are preparing themselves to take an aggressive action.

Q: In that connection, and this must have been of great concern to you, toward the end of the Eisenhower Administration I think it was estimated that 80 percent of the ships in the Navy would be obsolete in another five years, and we had only been building maybe 20 new ones a year because of costs and so forth. Was this a casualty?

Burke: Oh yes. But still we got more ships then we're getting now. We spent less money but the precentage of new ships was greater then.

Q: Did the President ever address himself to this subject?

Burke: Oh, yes. Oh, yes. I used to bring it up nearly every time I saw him.

Q: How did he react?

Burke: Well, he would consider it. And I fought--for example, he said that "Once I approve a budget I don't want you people going up there and undercutting my budget." Each time we'd say, "But Mr. President, what do we answer when they say, do you think this is enough? We'll say no. We've got to say no. We don't think it's enough."

He'd say, "You'd better be asked that question, you'd better not plant it either." Well, of course, it doesn't have to be planted, it's always asked.

Q: There's always going to be somebody asking that.

Burke: Yes. And so he would permit it very reluctantly. I had a statement that I wrote out very carefully, which I always read: "I do support the President's budget. But I think it would not be my way of building the budget. The priorities are different."

Q: He has the overall obligation . . .

Burke: Yes, he has the obligation. He has the authority,

the power and the obligation to take that action. "He has made a decision, I will support that decision—I don't think it's the right decision but I'll support it." Generally that's what it was. Now, the President didn't like that. No President does.

Q: What reaction did the committees give to that?

Burke: They said, all right, they bore right in on the question. Congress is wise and that's been going on for a good many centuries, I guess.

Interview with Admiral Arleigh Burke   Bethesda, Maryland
by John T. Mason, Jr.   November 24, 1972

Q: It's great of you to give me some more time today to discuss these years when you were Chief of Naval Operations and serving with President Eisenhower. Last time you talked somewhat about the President's concept of your duty as a member of the Joint Chiefs of Staff. You dwelt on that area of your activities to some extent, but I think you want to add something more today.

Admiral Burke: Yes, but first I want to thank you for coming out today, because I got tired of doing carpentry work after a couple of hours and it's a good change.

Well, President Eisenhower of course, wanted unanimous opinion from his Joint Chiefs, and this he always wanted because it was most distressing to him when we came up with what we called split papers, differing views on subjects, particularly within the services themselves, on a service matter. The differences of opinion were nearly always on missions or budgets or controls--who does it, who can do it best? Although he was insistent on that, he had a lot of split papers, because we had some very strong-minded Joint Chiefs.

Q: What percentage off hand were split papers?

Burke: Well, the percentage was very low overall, but the Joint Chiefs happened to have a tremendous number of papers, and the large number of them we did agree on, but many of those were comparatively unimportant. But on the real important papers, there was perhaps a 10 percent split, and this was quite a high percentage.

Now, I talked to President Eisenhower quite a few times, and I believe that the differences of opinion were sound. I was a member of the Joint Chiefs of Staff because I was brought up in the Navy. I knew the Navy capabilities and limitations, and I had a different concept of operations, a different concept of doing things than the ground services. We believed in mobility. We had to have mobility. We didn't have clear lines of demarcation between commanders. We depended upon commanders mutually supporting one another and doing their utmost to support. We didn't believe it was necessary to place a common commander over everybody and have the common commander direct all actions in detail. We believe he could call for help, call for assistance--ask another commander and get it. It works this way in the Navy very well. I had no objections during the war, for example, and several times I did work under a man who was quite a bit junior to me. When I was in destroyers, for example, there was a group of destroyers that got into battle, and I went up to reinforce him. He was already in battle. He knew what it was all about and I didn't, and so I took my orders from him, and he directed me on what to do to help him the most. This was commonplace and I thought nothing of it. Neither did anybody else.

I also thought that the Air Force Chief was brought up the same way. They'd had certain things that through a lifetime of experience they had learned from air combat, and it was a different thing. The Army, of course, I'd served quite a few periods with the Army at various times in my life and I knew a little bit about the Army, but the Army was completely different from either the Air Force or the Navy.

Well, the result was that every time we sent up a split paper, the President was very much concerned about it, and I tried to explain why I thought that it was good that he had to make the decision, because he was the man, the only man responsible for the whole United States. There was nobody else who was. And I thought this because our expertise was in different fields, but with common interests, so that it took the President, the President had to make the decision on where to spend his money, where to spend the government's money, where to put the emphasis. He had to have the unbiased direct advice of his military people to do this. He was a military man himself, but he was another one of those people who leaned over very much not to be a military man in the White House. He was less a military man in the White House than most any other President, because he feared--he didn't want to bring his military knowledge and his military methods of doing things into civilian government. He was right on that.

But I never could convince him that he should make-- that he really should make those decisions. They could not be made by the Joint Chiefs unless there were some weak Chiefs, unless there was back scratching among the Joint Chiefs. If you compromise, you compromise to get something that was not very good. Usually compromises of that kind are not very good.

Now, an example of that--the B-50 bomber, I did not believe that that was a good bomber. I believed that the Air Force should have bombers but I didn't think that particular bomber was a good buy, and the reason I thought this was that the Air Force was going for high altitude, high speed, and I thought, I was convinced that any missile could reach the altitude of any bomber, and any missile could go faster than a bomber, therefore, a high altitude level bomber was not very valuable. The higher it was, the farther it could be seen by radar, the easier it would be to be shot down if they had the missiles, and if the missiles weren't in existence then they soon would be.

What I thought the Air Force should have would be a high speed, low level bomber, so that when they made their attacks they could come down to the deck, and radars wouldn't be able to see them as far, and they'd have a greater chance of success.

Well, this was a technical thing. I talked it over with our own aviators. They agreed with my conclusion, but the Air Force didn't. Well, I fought the Air Force on that tooth and nail. I remember going down to Augusta one time, where the President was staying, a golf club, that's right, yes, he was down there, and we went down to see him on our budgets. And I thought I had him convinced--of course, the other Chiefs were there while I was making my speech-- I thought I had him convinced that he should cut the money from that bomber. The other Chiefs, of course, were very angry with me, or at least the Air Force Chief was.

But later on, he put some of the money back. Well, he sent for me and told me that he'd put it back as a compromise, he thought that the Air Force wanted that kind of a bomber, they believed in it, and although he could see my point of view, he didn't think it warranted cutting the whole thing out.

Well, they never did make that particular bomber, and later they found out this was right. But this distressed him, that he'd have to make that decision.

Q: What was it basically he was against in this area?

Burke: Well, he said more than once that if the Joint Chiefs can't make up their minds and jointly on all the problems that confront the military security of this country, then somebody else will make the decisions, and somebody else will make them up who doesn't know nearly as much about the military requirements as the Chiefs do.

Q: As long as he sat in that chair, he was the one who had to make the decisions and he did know.

Burke: Yes, he did know, so it wasn't a personal matter. He could do this, but he didn't like this system. Well, that's absolutely true, but the trouble is, that it's not just military security. You cannot separate military, economic, political affairs. They're all mixed up together, and somebody, and only the President can do it, has to make the decision as to what shall be done, how much of each kind of power there shall be and what the capabilities of that kind of power shall be and how it will be used. This is economic, political, psychological, all the other things that go into making up national power. But he also said that the Joint Chiefs should be strong minded but they should be able to come to a compromise, and I maintained that if the Joint Chiefs were really strong minded, they couldn't compromise on something that any individual thought was wrong.

Well, now, I still think I'm right, because you can see what's happened when you get Joint Chiefs that don't stand firmly on their position, as has happened in the past. One service gets a great deal more than they should, and you get into a strategy which is a compromise strategy, and a compromise strategy usually doesn't work.

For example, our strategy in Vietnam did not work, and it didn't work because it didn't follow what I think are the fundamentals of war. And the reason why they didn't was because either the Joint Chiefs agreed to something that I know individually they probably thought was wrong, or they had it imposed on them, I don't know which. But we lost the war because we didn't fight a war the way wars have to be fought in order to be won--that is, fighting in the enemy's territory, making him react to our initiative, doing all of those things that every generation has found necessary.

Q: You had to spend a great deal of time with the Joint Chiefs work, did you not, and if so, how did you manage your other hat as Chief of Naval Operations? Did you have to sluff off a lot on your deputies?

Burke: Oh yes, my Vice Chief. This is where I was most fortunate. When I became Chief of Naval Operations, I didn't change the organization nor did I change the people in it very fast, and I inherited from Admiral Carney a very fine man who was much older than I was, a very experienced, quiet individual, Admiral Duncan, as Vice Chief. He was slow. He did not like change very much.

Q: Is this Admiral Wu Duncan?

Burke: Admiral Wu Duncan. He had some characteristics that bothered a lot of people, but he was very certain--he would not do anything until he was quite sure that it was the proper thing to do, and he kept advising me all the time not to make changes, not to destroy anything until I found a replacement for it--in other words, not to eliminate something until I was sure either that it wasn't needed at all or that the substitute would work, because otherwise you just keep the Navy in a state of flux. Well, he was right on that.

So he was wonderful. He stayed for a little while and then I looked around to find a man who would disagree with me, because the head of any organization is a lonesome individual. You have to make a lot of decisions. You have to make decisions just like the President, but on a much lesser scale, among various proposals, and I needed somebody that would disagree with me but who was straightforward and had great integrity and would--and great experience, too. I didn't want just a stubborn man, but I wanted somebody who was very intelligent, from a different background, different personal characteristics, so that I could discuss matters with him.

Q: You wanted somebody who would complement you and your personality.

Burke: Yes. I knew that was an unpleasant thing to be. It's not an easy way to operate. But I'd seen people in CNO and other high places where they had a group of yes men around them and they'd never worked out very well, unless the man himself is very brilliant, because no man knows that much. So I needed somebody to make sure that we didn't make any serious mistakes, or if we made them, I would not make them without knowing that somebody thought it was a serious mistake.

So I looked all over the whole flag list in the Navy, and I came on a very happy choice in (Admiral) Don Felt. Don was an aviator, a small, irascible individual, hard-headed and tough man, and he and I used to have a lot of very big arguments, but he was extremely loyal to the Navy which is what you want. He was knowledgeable. He had his nose to the grindstone, and he would carry out things or tell me that he hadn't exactly the way I thought they should be carried out. He kept me fully informed. He really ran the detail of the Navy, but he kept me informed so that I could make the decisions that I should make. We had a very successful operation going. Now, it wasn't pleasant. It isn't pleasant to fight continuously with a good friend, and after a while you wonder whether he's all that good, that good a friend, and I know it was unpleasant for Don, too. But it operated extremely well.

Q: That was the way you looked at the job and it had to be done.

Burke: Yes. He was extremely good. Later--of course, you can only keep a man in that position so long, because he wears out and after a while you have a doubt as to whether or not this opposition is just a habit or whether he really thinks that way, and so after a couple of years, Don--when CincPac opened up, Don was the ideal man for that because he was a very hard working excellent naval officer, and I couldn't hold him back just selfishly to keep him in the

Vice Chief's job. So he got CincPac, and I got another man who was just like Don, different personal characteristics, but he was an aviator, hard-headed, experienced, good war record, in Jim Russell. They were both--those were two of the best appointments I ever made, in those two people, because they did an awful lot for the Navy. They ran the routine.

Q: And freed you for the--

Burke: --freed me and also gave me advice on Joint Chiefs affairs. I wouldn't take a position on a Joint Chiefs of Staff paper, on an important matter, unless I discussed it with them, the Vice Chief, and also the deputies and most of the time the action officers way down, because they were the experts in those matters, the action people, and the rest of us, we brought our differing experiences to bear on the problem, and we could usually arrive at a pretty sound decision.

I got this thing of having somebody opposed to me during the war, because when I went off to the Pacific, went out on a transport and I had lots of time to study, and I studied the battle reports I'd gotten in San Francisco, all that I could, and I found that nearly all the commanders were making decisions, they had to make them very fast, but they didn't have anybody to tell them what the probable pitfalls of their decisions might be. And so--

Q: --it takes time to see those things.

Burke: It takes time to see them, and it takes somebody to think of what's wrong with this, instead of how to do it, and so one time, I was down in Purvis Bay in the Solomons and a big man came over, said he was from the PT boats and he wanted to go with me because the PT boat war was pretty much over, he thought, in that area and he wanted to go with me. It turned out to be Whizzer White, and I said, "Fine, you can come aboard and be my intelligence officer."

He said, "You rate an intelligence officer?" I said, "No I don't, but I'll --

He said, "When do I come?" I said, "Now." He said, "I don't have any clothes." I said, "If that bothers you don't bother to come."

Well, we went up the slot that afternoon, and of course, he was wonderful. When I went to carriers I took him with me. His main job besides riding the intelligence circuits, which gave us a lot of valuable information, his main job was to criticize what I was going to do. I explained every action if I had time, and I always had time, I think I did, to tell him what I was going to do and he'd criticize it. I got so that I dreaded listening to his criticism just before the battle. Sometimes it would take only a minute or two. I dreaded that more than I did fighting the battle. Because--

Q: --He was going to take the negative point of view.

Burke: He was going to take the negative point of view. I did what I wanted to do, but he could point out where I might make a mistake.

Q: That gave you another dimension.

Burke: It gave me another dimension. And also sometimes I changed. Sometimes I found out--he'd say, "Don't drive in so close." For example, I'd tell him, "I'm going to get 45 degrees on the bow of the enemy, I'm going in to 4000 yards, I'm going to fire torpedoes and turn right, retire to 9000 yards, then open fire with guns."

He'd say, "Don't do it, 4000 yards, you're on the wrong course for that, your moon 'll be behind you, make it 5000."

Well, those things helped. Or he'd say, "You can drive in closer." Those were tactical things. He could also tell me that, "If you hit a big--this group of ships that you think are--there may be more. I think, although you've been told there are three ships, from reading intelligence reports there may be six, be prepared for six, I don't think you ought to go in with all you've got at the beginning."

This is one of the reasons why I developed the tactics I used of having one division to stand by, to come in hard right now, while the other division was fighting, so you could always have one division as a surprise for the enemy. You might not surprise him but--

Q: --When you were more sure of the enemy--

Burke: Yes, one outfit to engage him and the other outfit could attack, could stand by to take you off the hook in case you got into trouble.

Q: Admiral, it's hard to come by a mind like that, a person like that.

Burke: Well, of course, White is a wonderful man.

Q: Then it really depends on your ability to judge a man and judge him quickly, I supposed, as to his capability.

Burke: No. I was lucky on that. There's no way you can

tell. I used to think I could pick men pretty well, but I made a couple of mistakes. I was certainly lucky on those people. They were marvelous. And there's an awful lot of things we did, that I got credit for in CNO, that shouldn't be credited to any individual, but to a group of people who made sure that I had the word.

Q: Last time you told me that President Eisenhower was constantly encouraging you and the other Chiefs to go ahead with the development on conventional weapons, in contrast with the atomic.

Burke: Well, I think the President realized more than anybody else in the whole world the awfulness, awesomeness, I guess, of nuclear warfare, and although due to progress on technical things, nuclear warfare was possible, that if it came about there would be a complete nation destroyed or nearly destroyed. It was very valuable--our nuclear power was very valuable to keep the USSR from aggressing and nothing else would have probably at that time. And it if hadn't been for nuclear power, it's very likely that the Soviet Union would have been able to take over more of Western Europe. And yet at the same time, nuclear power was new. The Air Force particularly thought that they could do everything with just nuclear power.

They wanted to just threaten to destroy a nation and have the ability to destroy a nation, no matter what they did, and that they would not commit aggression and they would do things that we felt, the United States felt and other "free world" nations felt should be done.

Well, the President knew that wasn't true. Just as Dulles had said in one of his speeches, you've got to make the punishment fit the crime, and if the Soviet Union took a small piece of territory, how big a piece would it have to be before you'd launch?

They recognized the power, the limitations of that kind of power. That was all or nothing, nuclear power. So the President said, "We've got to have a military force that can handle any situation. And that means, in a small situation we've got to have the proper equipment and proper plans to correct it, and it doesn't mean that we will have to launch for everything."

This was countering the Air Force philosophy at that time. So we were, of course, fighting hard to get nuclear weapons in carriers. We had nuclear weapons in carriers. We were fighting hard to get the kinds of nuclear weapons that would be effective, the smaller ones, that we could handle.

During that time also we developed Polaris which

was only nuclear and could only be used to destroy--for big events.

Q: That's in the category of the Ultimate Weapon.

Burke: The Ultimate Weapon. So he kept stressing that you've got to have conventional weapons too. Of course, I believed that, so did the Army. The Air Force did not, in general. They didn't. Because the Army and the Navy were trying to get the lesser weapons, torpedoes, better guns, better electronic gear, better surface to air missiles, using conventional explosives--most of his effort was on convincing the Air Force that they should have tactical weapons, tactical support.

Q: He recognized he didn't have to convince you and the Army.

Burke: Yes, although he gave us all the lecture.

Q: Where would he do this, National Defense Council?

Burke: In the White House--no, usually just the Chiefs. For example, he wanted--he suggested, that the Air Force should have bombers capable of carrying conventional weapons. The Air Force didn't think so. But after he was out of the Presidency, in the Vietnam War, the B-52's which were built solely for delivery of nuclear weapons were modified to carry conventional high explosive weapons. This is what he had in mind.

We also had some difficulty in the expense of weapons, even at that time weapons systems were getting so sophisticated that they were becoming more expensive and consequently you couldn't get as many as you probably would need. So we were all endeavoring to get something that would do and wouldn't cost so much. Well, this is a very hard thing to determine. Take in the Vietnam War, there at the beginning, we could have used some World War II airplanes very, very well. They cost maybe one-tenth as much as the planes did at the beginning of Vietnam, at that time.

Well, manufacturers weren't tooled up to make them, would have to start all over again. But those World War II aircraft would not have done the job against modern aircraft, if they had to fight modern aircraft they wouldn't have done it at all. They couldn't stand up against any of the Migs, but they would have done very well --

Q: Against the ground defences too.

Burke: Not the ground defences that are there now, but they could have at the beginning. Well, it's a question of keeping some inexpensive weapons, a mix between inexpensive weapons and very sophisticated weapons. I still think that the military quite frequently wants the most sophisticated, the very best weapon it can get, but it costs so much that they can't get enough of them, and somehow a compromise has got to be made farther down the line, to have some weapons that don't cost so much, can't do all the things that your very best weapons can do.

Q: What impact did this policy of the President's have in the Navy on the R and D program?

Burke: Well, not very much because we were--we had a pretty heavy R and D program anyway. R and D is a very hard thing to get by or was a very hard thing to get by our civilian superiors, because they would want to know, "What are you going to come out with?"

We didn't know, on basic research. It is a pioneering area. Now, the applied research was something else again. There we could do research--well, this was like Polaris. All the research that was done on Polaris was really applied research, where you only go a little bit beyond the state of the art, and you can achieve success. But the research on torpedoes, for example, is a state of the art application, but they--our torpedoes now are extremely expensive and they can do wonderful things, if you have enough of them. Maybe we ought to do some research on cheapening the torpedo and having 80 percent or 90 percent effective--still, we had some very terrible experiences at the beginning of World War II when torpedoes wouldn't work.

Q: That prompts me to ask you, do you envision the time when modern weaponry becomes so expensive that you'll simply have to be content with lesser things?

Burke: Well, yes. Yes, I do. You go back to knives again--the use of knives. Here we are in Vietnam, fighting a very small nation, with very little productive power, supported by two big nations who do have productive power, but they did not have initially any sophisticated weapons at all. They had only hand carried weapons and unsophisticated World War II type weapons. So what did they do? How can you win like that? Well, you win, as Mao Tse-tung said, you win by protracted conflict and infiltration, and you seek the type of conflict where sophisticated weapons cannot be used effectively.

Q: You don't take on a first rate power?

Burke: You can take on a first rate power, but not--but you do it through guerilla warfare, you do it through infiltration, you do it through changing the --

What's normally called, unconventional warfare. Also you use political means. For example, the political means which has been used against us, in trying to convince our people not to fight a war, that the war is wrong, that we are doing the wrong thing, and you get dissension in your enemy's camp, you do it by convincing, indirectly, maybe through spies, through agents, to conduct a war--a part time war, such as we did in Vietnam, by not attacking the enemy lots of times, by not doing those things which are necessary to win a war. In other words, we went for a no-win war, unfortunately, a bad expression but still I think it's generally true.

So it's going to be necessary to have conventional weapons. Well, before I say that, the North Vietnamese have used men instead of equipment. They have lost men, a lot of men, a lot more than we have. They would send in a platoon or company or regiment and lose a great many of them, in a good aggressive attack. We would not do that. We couldn't take that sort of punishment at the moment. So we have all sorts of equipment to take the place of men.

Now, in a showdown eventually, you can't have anything to take the place of men. War is unfortunately a vicious terrible thing, but it depends on the willingness of men to fight for a system of government, for a cause which they believe justifies their death, that they're willing to sacrifice themselves for. If you don't have that, in the long run then the nation crumbles.

We got our independence because we believed that. All of our wars we fought with that condition, except perhaps the Vietnam War.

There's an old story that was told about the Middle East years ago, probably before Christ, that periodically the men on the plains get soft and complacent and affluent, and the men in the hills that are rugged, hard men, the men from the hills come down and destroy the men on the plains, and drive the men on the plains away and they take over the plains. And the men that used to be on the plains go back to the hills. After two or three generations, they are the rugged ones and the thing is repeated.

There may be something to that, because although, no matter how much theory there is, how much you would like to see war done away with and a system established so that people could get along with one another without fighting, without competition, without conflict, it doesn't happen that way. It never has happened that way, probably never will.

And so sometimes men who are willing to sacrifice,

or a society that is willing to sacrifice, willing to defend and maybe attack for what they believe, can take over, even though their system of government, even though their ideas are wrong, or at least some people think they're wrong. This is why Communism--this is the strength of Communism, not that the Communist system is good, but because the Communists are ruthless enough or have been ruthless enough up to now to demand absolute loyalty to their cause or at least absolute obedience, and they get it. And they are willing to fight, and if they don't fight, they shoot their people. They chain them to gun carriages and things like that, but they get a very effective combat force out of that.

Q: Somewhere in that picture, Admiral, is it not true that the concept of the worth of the individual comes into play?

Burke: Yes, this is right. We have gone very far in believing that there is nothing more important than a man's life, and yet we were talking about Herb Riley and other people just before. Every man knows he's going to die, and it's good to die for something that you believe to be important. If a man just dies and lives a long life and accomplishes nothing and then he dies anyway, and what has he done? He must not have any sense of great achievement. Other people who do want to do something sometimes die in the process of doing it. But they die, I think, with some sense of achievement. And those people who do something and risk their lives and then later die, at least they have a little sense of achievement, that they've done something for a cause that they believe in.

Q: I was thinking in terms of our own attitude and the development of weapons to save manpower, in contrast with the Vietnamese who just threw masses of men in because human life is considered cheap by them.

Burke: Yes, that's right, and we probably over-value human life and they under-value it. Nobody wants to lose his troops. But this has caused a lot of argument throughout history, from time immemorial, of a commander who throws in his troops recklessly, as - say, in a frontal attack, and some of them have. They haven't gained much. But sometimes commanders have thrown in all their troops, taken very heavy losses on a frontal attack, and succeeded, where if they had fought a slow war or an attrition war, they would have lost more troops in the long run and perhaps would have failed. It's a question again of tactics, mostly tactics but sometimes strategy, what to do, and commanders make mistakes.

But certainly if a society is not willing, the individuals of a society are not willing to risk their life for their society, then the society can't exist. Somebody else--some other society will take it over.

Q: Admiral, the other day you told me that partly as a result of your (-- you didn't say it but I say it,) demonstration of your mettle, that incident which involved the Secretaries of Defense and Navy with whom you differed on personnel policy, you said as a result the President got in the habit of calling you over to the White House occasionally in the late afternoon, and he would use you as something of a sounding board, perhaps he would pick your mind on subjects which weren't always military subjects but which were subjects that he was concerned with at that time. Can you recall some of those instances?

Burke: Yes, but first, I wasn't--I probably overstated it. I wasn't chief advisor to the President.

Q: You made the point that you were not the only one he did this with, but he certainly didn't do it just generally speaking with everybody. He picked out his men.

Burke: Well, the President needs unbiased opinions sometimes, and sometimes an unbiased opinion of somebody who isn't very close to a specific problem is valuable. Sometimes he just needs to assure himself that he is really on the right track in general, without specifics. Everybody--not everybody, a great many people have the tendency to tell the President or the ruler of a country what he would like to hear. They know his general ideas--They read enough of what he thinks, and there's a great tendency to tell him what he wants to hear.

Q: In effect, it's currying favor.

Burke: In a way, but more than that, they have a great respect and a little awe of the office, maybe a lot of awe of the office, and they don't want to argue with somebody--they don't want to cause the President to be unhappy and they don't want to argue with somebody who may know more about it than they know, and they don't--so the President is in a difficult spot of having people to tell him what they really believe. And it's very hard to get people like that. Every organization has the same thing.

So first, of course, when the President would send for me, it was usually on some military problem or some problem associated with the military. In other words, he said, "The Army wants to do this. They want to change the type of their division. They want to do this and this is the way it is now. What do you think about it?

Well, I wouldn't know very much about that, but sometimes I could give him a general idea of something. Other things--then, the most usual matter was some international relations problem, something having to do with the State Department's work--that is, what do you think is going to happen in Egypt? What should we do in Egypt? Do you think we should give them a lot of aid to help Egypt? Do you think it will help any? Will that help them come to our side? How do you think we should do it?

Q: Was that a specific--

Burke: Yes, that was one, on Egypt.

Q: It involved the Aswan Dam?

Burke: No, not the Aswan Dam, not that one because the Aswan Dam was Mr. Dulles's affair primarily. But aid in general.

Another one that caught me completely by surprise was taxation. Yes, the President felt--oh, the last year or so he was in office, he was concerned about the increasing costs of government and inflation, and our balance of payments. This worried him a great deal, the economic situation of the country, and particularly the balance of payments at one time, and he asked me whether I thought that the balance of payments, how the balance of payments could be cured, and whether the steps that other people had suggested should be taken or not, to have a balance of payments. Those steps were to bring some of the troops home, to increase our rate of productivity by not letting inflation go up, not letting wages go up, and, of course, I was all for that. He didn't do it. It was too complicated a problem. It's getting worse every year. But he was very much concerned about the economic situation, and he was right. He did balance the budget at times and he tried very hard to always keep the budget in balance. I believe that a nation should not be in debt even to its own people very much. That is, a debt that goes beyond twice the annual income of a nation is very heavy debt, and if it gets too heavy, it can't be paid. If it can't be paid some day, something's going to crumble.

Now, this is something I didn't know anything at all about, but--

Q: You knew it in terms of family income, debt and so forth, knew it in that sense, and isn't that just a microcosm of the other problem?

Burke: No. No, because the family can't print money, the government can. The family can't obligate itself beyond--

people won't let it be obligated. I mean, you can't borrow money indefinitely because people won't loan it to you, but a government can borrow all the money that it wants, until it cracks.

Q: Admiral, you said off tape that there was another area that he was concerned about and talked with you about.

Burke: Sometimes he would ask my opinion of an individual, particularly once in a while when he had a vacancy that he wanted to fill, because he was a man, I think probably like all Presidents, what he wanted to do was to get people of great integrity in there, in all the important positions. It's the most important thing there is. But also somebody that had administrative experience, and he checked pretty carefully, through a great many people, on what they heard about it, so that he didn't appoint somebody that he didn't know much about.

Q: You said earlier, talking about the economic issues, and the question of bringing troops home from Europe--what was your position on that, and did you express yourself?

Burke: Yes. What I thought should be done was to bring them home slowly. Sooner or later, our troops in Europe have got to come back, all of them. We aren't going to have troops there a hundred years from now and we probably won't have troops there 50 years from now, so some day they're going to come back. Well, you can't just suddenly say, "I'm going to bring all the troops back next week or next month or next year," and you can't do it without conferring with the other nations, so what I thought should be done would be to have a conference with the other nations and say, "We're going to bring back our troops some day. Now, let's discuss when they should all be out of there, and agree to a date that's satisfactory to most everybody, and then let us discuss the rate at which we bring them back, when we start, and we'll make a plan for bringing our troops back. Of course, that plan can be changed at any time, but still we'll have a general goal towards which we can work." I thought perhaps if he were to do that, the plan might end up that in ten years we'd have our troops out, and that we would take maybe 10 percent per year, and that could be studied by the people. We wouldn't propose initially any specific plan but would let that develop. It didn't matter much what the plan was in detail, so long as there was a plan for eventually getting them out. He thought so too, but again it was something that was never done because nobody wanted to go farther than one or two years, and you can't do this in a hurry.

Q: Wasn't it contingent also on the state of the cold war?

Burke: Sure and that would be what would modify it, but still he wanted to bring them back. There were always pressures, don't bring them back now, we'll bring them back next year or two years from now. In this a long range plan would have been, I thought, valuable.

Q: You touched on the Suez situation but used it as an illustration of the Dulles concept, the use of power. I wonder if you'd develop the picture a little more thoroughly today and bring the President in on it and his attitude toward the whole situation?

Burke: Well, of course, this is all from memory and I haven't even read about this for probably ten years, but I think--the Suez problem was getting worse all the time. We had promised, United States had promised to build an Aswan Dam. I don't know whether we really promised or they just thought we had promised. In any case, the Egyptians were getting recalcitrant, and we, United States official position was that the British were pressing too hard, pressing the Egyptians too hard and the Egyptians were demanding too much.

We withdrew our support from the Aswan Dam and the

Egyptians got out of hand. They closed the Suez Canal and the British were going to do something about it. The British didn't tell us what they were going to do. They didn't inform the government, at least I don't think they did, I didn't know anything about it. But they suddenly (to the US) decided to attack Egypt, with French support, and they did not give their services, particularly Navy and Air Force, sufficient warning to be ready for the operation which was necessary. That was a difficult operation. So it was obvious that the British were not going to be able to conduct a real good operation, and that the success of their operation would depend a good deal on the support that the United States gave them.

Well, the British didn't tell us anything about it. They kept it secret from us. They were manipulating without asking for our help or informing us of it, and that, of course, made our governmental officials in State, Mr. Dulles, angry. It probably also made the President angry. I don't know. But in any case, I thought that we should help the British a little bit, at least give them good strong moral support. We didn't.

As soon as this thing started, I sent the Sixth Fleet to sea, and I sent orders to Cat Brown who commanded the Sixth fleet then to be sure he was prepared for action, to keep his ships disposed so they could go into battle, and to keep his troops trained all ready so that he would be all set.

So he sent back, "Roger, but who's the enemy?"

That's when I sent him the dispatch, "I don't know, we won't take any guff from anyone."

Well, he was at sea not knowing whether to support the British--I didn't know either--or whether to try to stop the British. Newspaper reports indicated we were oppossing the landing, and we did, opposed the operation of the British and the French. So old Cat, he didn't know what to do. And I didn't know what to tell him.

But this was a question then--I think now that we were wrong in not supporting the British, even though they did do a lot of things that were quite bad, but it would have been better not to have let that operation fail, and we did.

Q: Did you advise the President when you gave the order to alert the Sixth Fleet?

Burke: Oh, yes. Oh, yes, he got all the information.

Q: Did he have any immediate reaction?

Burke: No. It was the proper thing to do, when somebody's

going to conduct a fight you've got to be ready for it.

Q: Did you have any meeting with him during the time that this crisis was in being?

Burke: Oh yes, I'm sure we did. All the Chiefs did. Quite frequently, probably every day or every other day. But I don't remember now anything specific happening. In my records I'm sure there are--There's a lot of data, but I don't remember it. I do remember that I wanted to give the British some amphibious support and landing craft, things like that.

Q: Another area that the Navy was heavily involved in was in the development of guided missiles prior to the development of the Polaris itself. I wondered if you'd talk about that area and how the President may have gotten involved in it, what his attitude was towards this program of the Navy?

Burke: Yes. Well, to go back a little bit, I took chemical engineering at Michigan and specialized in explosives.

Q: This was PG.

Burke: PG, yes. So I'd been interested in missiles and propellants for a long time, and after the war I was made chief of research of the Bureau of Ordnance, so at that time our chief missile developer was John Hopkins University JPL.

They were trying to develop ram jets, and they were developing surface to air missiles. They had a forerunner of the TERRIER then. It wasn't very good. In development. So when I became Chief of Research the TERRIER was--had been developed. It wasn't a very accurate weapon or a very reliable one. We did not have surface to surface missiles, except what really was a converted airplane or REGULUS. We had converted a submarine to carry the REGULUS and--yes, this is REGULUS I, and it was, what it was was an unmanned aircraft in effect. What we needed mostly at that time was a surface to air missile to shoot down airplanes which might attack the Fleet. So we emphasized that. We developed a family of close-in surface to air missiles, then medium missiles, the TERRIER, then long range missiles which was TALOS. They were all similar, but they could not be used on the same mount, nor were they--they were not interchangeable though some of the gear, some of the components were interchangeable. We were trying to develop a single missile that would do all the jobs, still would not be too expensive, and be accurate and be reliable.

We spent a lot of money on this, and it was very hard getting that money, and each time we had to--I had to defend this with the Bureau of the Budget or the President, also before Congress. But the President was not very missile-minded in the beginning. I think by the time he left office, he was. But he couldn't see, it was very difficult for him to see why we needed so very much money to develop a surface to air missile. He could see the need for the missile all right but he couldn't understand why it cost so much, and as a matter of fact it did cost a tremendous amount, but you cannot invent on schedule nor can you invent on a specific amount. We did make a great many improvements, and we did develop them so they were put on as the main armament on a great many frigates and destroyers during that time.

Now, the air to air missile, we'd (all services) had several air to air missiles, none of them very good, and I heard indirectly of a man out in Inyokern who had developed, who was trying to develop an air to air missile on his own. This was Dr. McLean. And I asked how he was coming, what he was trying to do, and I found he was doing this in quite a bit of his spare time and also a little government time, and he needed some money, so we gave him a little bit of money, I think $50,000 and he developed SIDEWINDER. It was a very good simple air to air missile. It's still being used. Even the first ones were very good.

This showed that sometimes something very important is developed by a single man who has an idea, and he doesn't have laboratory support nor does he have any support at all but he can develop a very useful weapons system. This was very cheap. The development cost very little and production cost very little, and it's a very good missile still.

Q: Admiral Withington considers it one of the greatest developments during his regime in BuOrd.

Burke: Yes. Well, it was. McLean did a very fine job.

Q: REGULUS II was coming along.

Burke: Yes, REGULUS II was coming along and in that we had hopes for a good surface to surface missile, but it was big. It was big. It took a lot of space and it took some time to prepare it to fire, quite a while to prepare it to fire. It wasn't something that you could shoot in ten seconds. But it was a guided missile, and we were developing it, but it cost a great deal of money, and the Air Force and the Army both and a lot of other people opposed REGULUS II. Finally they cut it out of the budget, which was a tremendous mistake--not that REGULUS II would ever have amounted to anything as such, but if we had kept on surface to surface missiles, guided missiles, we could have developed something, a successor to REGULUS II that would have been an effective weapon.

Q: Something comparable to what the Russians did?

Burke: The Russians did this with the STIX. As a matter of fact, they took a cheap REGULUS II and made a very good missile out of it, and we would have probably done the same thing. We are still right now trying to develop a surface to surface missile that's equal to the STIX. We have it now, but we should have been far in advance if we'd kept up the research on that sort of thing. This just shows that a weapons system that can be conceived should be worked on, in particular if there's a void such as there is against surface ships--there's a void there now, how are you going to sink them (enemy ships)? And a surface to surface guided missile will do it. That should have been enough for us to do research on it, but we didn't do it.

Q: You simply can't break off and resume at a later date.

Burke: No. You lose years, and you lose the people who are interested in it. They go to some other job. They get into something else. So you have to get a whole new team to develop it.

Q: I assume you fought for the continuance of REGULUS.

Burke: Yes, I thought REGULUS II was a very important missile. But I lost that one.

Q: Couldn't get the President on your side?

Burke: No. No. He made many of his decisions, as Presidents always do, depending upon the advice he got from a lot of people, and nearly everybody was advising him against it except for the Navy. We were a lone voice, and we didn't win that one.

I guess it was actually killed while I was in office, but it may not have been for a year or so later.

Q: It was a casualty really of the Polaris program, wasn't it, when the Navy had to put all their eggs in that basket.

Burke: Yes, it was because we had to divert the money, probably. We could only get so much money, and that was a casualty of that.

Q: From what you say about the REGULUS and an earlier statement, I draw the implication that the President wasn't totally appreciative of the value of research and development programs.

Burke: Well, I think that's probably true of any head of any concern. I'm on the board of Texaco, for example, and research people always feel that they aren't getting quite the support that they should have, and there's some truth to it. It's true of every concern that I'm with. Research always feels they're being short-changed. Now, I don't think they actually are, because a company or a nation cannot put all their money in research. You have to develop something sometimes. You have to get a piece of hardware that will work, and you can't just do research, and if it becomes a question of when do you cut it, when have you done enough research on this and you start putting it into production?

Q: But in the realm of business and industry, one learns that the company that one should consider investing in is the one that has an extensive research program under way, there's a relationship.

Burke: Yes. there's a relationship, but there's also the thing in government that just putting money into research doesn't do the job. You've got to have the right people to do the job, and a mediocre engineer, no matter how many mediocre people you have on research, you'll not get very much out of it. But if you can have a very few excellent people, you can get a lot more out of it for a lot less money. Now, the question is, how do you find a man who's good in research? How do you know that? Governmental laboratories have done a marvelous job, but they have a reputation which is not quite deserved of having too many mediocre people in them.

Q: In this same area, in the year 1957, when Secretary

McElroy succeeded Wilson as Secretary of Defense, it was in October of that year that the Soviets launched their first man-made satellite. McElroy took note of this whole thing and tried to put more emphasis on research in that area. He insisted upon more money for basic research. Did you get involved in that?

Burke: Oh yes, we got involved in it. We always--we lost the battle of launching, for launching space vehicles from sea. We wanted to do that because we thought we could build a good sea launching platform for medium-sized missiles, that it could be moved around and take advantage of launching from various places. But we didn't get very much money for it. We did a few. We did a little bit of research on it. That's when we started, about then is when we started our navigational satellites. We shifted then to satellite work, putting things in the vehicles rather than trying to launch the vehicle. Obviously there wasn't enough money--the ground launching system cost so very much that there wasn't going to be any money left over for other launching systems.

Q: In the light of what you said about missiles and research work under way not only in the Navy but elsewhere, what comment can you make on the charge which came up in the later Presidential campaign about a missile gap?

Burke: Oh, the missile gap--the missile gap was caused by an interpretation of intelligence. At that time every service had its own technical intelligence. There was the Central Intelligence Agency which gathered a great deal of information, but mostly political information, but the services, each service had its own very good intelligence system. But there was great difficulty in evaluating what, the fragments of information that each of the services got as to what the Russians were doing. The Air Force always over-estimated the number of missiles that the Soviets had. They added all the little points up, all the indications that would indicate that the Russians were building lots of missiles, and they always evaluated it so that they (Soviets) would be making more progress than they actually were doing, as it turned out later.

Army took a good deal of the same data, and they made estimates that were always on the low side, the lowest of the three. Ours, the Navy's estimates were usually in between but closer to the Army's than to the Air Force's.

Now, the CIA usually took a mean, not exactly--but it's impossible to tell exactly what the Russians are doing, and they were all estimates. But the politicians decided that there--the Democrats at that time--that there was a great big missile gap. They took the Air Force data and indicated that there was a great big missile gap, and they stressed this.

Q: Did this have any relationship to Senator Symington?

Burke: Oh yes, Symington was the leader of this thing. Well, actually, as it turned out, all of the figures, all of the estimates that we had before then were high. The Soviets were farther behind even than any of us thought they were. And within a very few months after the Democrats took over, after they won office, they found that there was no missile gap at all, and when it came time for the missile crisis, the President knew very well (that is in Cuba) that the Soviets had very few missiles in existence. So he could act with complete assurance that it was not possible for the Soviets to launch an all out attack against the United States. They didn't have the missiles. So the missile gap was a political fiction, based on interpreting all one way.

Now, this sounds as if the Air Force was horrible in doing this. This is the advantage of having the three services with differences of opinion. It turned out we were all--none of us were very accurate. But if the Air Force figures were taken, we would act on assumptions that were completely wrong, without any checks. And that's what the

Democrats did. But making plans on something like that, other than political plans, is a very dangerous thing.

Now they have just one DOD intelligence system, and the answer that they get is the only answer that you have, and you don't have any checks on it. No matter how hard a man tries, he's got to have different interpretations of fragmentary information. You can't get it exact.

Q: That came into being after you left office, did it not?

Burke: Yes. That was not while I was there. I had a good example of this intelligence business when I was out in the Korean War. We had--ComNavFe when I was Deputy Chief of Staff had four, I think four officers out on their intelligence staff, and they told me one morning, "It looks to us like the Chinese are in North Korea." They gave me the fragments of information. Fine, so we had a meeting every morning at 8 o'clock over at CincUNK, intelligence briefing, and so afterwards, after the briefing I went to see (General) Willoughby who was G-2 and told him, "My people think that the Chinese are in, because of these reasons."

Willoughby said, "Let's call the people in," so he called the chiefs of his sections in. They discussed the matter, and they didn't think the Chinese were in Korea. Same information we got, raw intelligence, but a question of a difference of interpretation.

Then Willoughby made a mistake. He said, "I don't think they're in there either." He looked at the date, "I don't think they're in there either, and I don't think they will come in."

Well, I went back and told my people, "They don't think so." "Well, maybe they aren't in, we don't know."

Two or three days later they got more information, little more fragments, and they said, "Well, we think they're in." So I went over to Willoughby again and we went over it again, and again they didn't think so, but at that time, I thought they were. So I sent a dispatch back to Admiral Sherman who was CNO then and said that I intended to keep (with Admiral Joy's approval I did this)--that I intended to keep every fifth transport, after it was unloaded, in case they did come in.

Q: That was based on your earlier theory, in the Solomons.

Burke: Yes. Well, by the time the Chinese were in there, it was definitely proved they were in there, we had 90 transports, and we could evacuate Hungnam, which we could never have evacuated--never could have carried out that operation unless we'd had those ships.

Well, this shows that a very few people, but just in--

terpreting the facts differently--these were very fragmentary pieces of information that they had--and not that Willoughby was wrong in his evaluation or that we were right, but it's two different interpretations, and Willoughby made the mistake of saying he didn't think they would come in at all, when he should have said, "Let's follow this thing very carefully because they may be right." And I didn't insist on it either. But our (Navy) people did happen to evaluate it correctly, and the intentions or capabilities of what an enemy is going to do are based upon very small bits of information, a great deal of which is inaccurate.

Q: So you make the point that the commander on our side is better off if there are different interpretations that he has to deal with rather than one single one that's definitive.

Burke: Yes, that's right, and he can tell from experience with his people which one is probably the most nearly accurate, by past records.

Q: At least it makes him a little more cautious in taking action.

Burke: Yes. He gets a spread of data. And he's got to be prepared for both ends of it, both extremes.

Q: Going back to the so-called missile gap, President Eisenhower in '57 some time or other, in November, began a series of television appearances which were intended to instruct the people on our advances in missilery and so forth, but he had to call it short because of his attack. Would this have dispelled this later charge, if he had been able to go through with this series? Was he intending to develop it to that extent?

Burke: I don't know, and I doubt if it would have made very much difference, because political parties want to get a hold on an issue, and that turned out to be a good issue, even though it was completely fictitious. I think it probably would still have been an issue.

Q: In that same area, in the year 1958, the Navy sent up its VANGUARD I. Do you want to talk about that?

Burke: Well, VANGUARD I was the initial missile in orbit. It was a little bit of a thing that we put into orbit, and after we got it into orbit, it sent its signals and there was no self-destruct thing in the VANGUARD, in the little satellite, so we said that it probably will go beeping around there for a couple of thousand years. Actually it didn't last quite that long. But we were far advanced then. We were a little bit ahead of the other services.

Q: The Army had the EXPLORER.

Burke: Army had the EXPLORER, right. They had bigger missiles. VANGUARD was a very small one. We put up I think it was three VANGUARD missiles before the Army got their big missile, their bigger payload up there. Of course, the VANGUARD was so small, it didn't have enough payload. But we thought we should be permitted to continue, but we were not permitted to continue in VANGUARD. They killed that, because they wanted to put it all into one launcher, and they probably were right, looking back on it.

Q: This was a Department of Defense decision.

Burke: Yes.

Q: You must have been thrilled at the VANGUARD, however.

Burke: Oh yes. It was a very happy thing. Very. And they did a marvelous job on it, because we didn't have many people on that job. It was a very small outfit developed that. They did a marvelous job.

Q: You were an old hand at dealing with proposals for reorganization of the Defense Department, having been involved originally in the Truman Administration. The subject came up again in the Eisenhower Administration, 1958, when the President himself proposed changes, and there was a measure finally enacted by the Congress. Would you tell me about your role in that?

Burke: Well, I opposed that all the way, because I felt that the President could use authority that he already had to reorganize the Defense Department to improve it without requiring a lot more authority which later could be used to make a single service or single chief of staff concept come true.

Q: What was his purpose, Sir, if he already had sufficient authority why was he seeking more at that time?

Burke: Well, I never quite understood it, but I think that he wanted a mandate from Congress to go ahead and do what he wanted to do, and so he wanted to get the authority to do very specific things, most of which he could have done without changing the law, but which by changing the law gave subsequent people more authority than he wanted to use.

Q: Was it related in any way to the studies former President Hoover had made on government?

Burke: Yes. There's always a tendency when anything in a big organization, to want to run it, to want to centralize it. --And Mr. Hoover did this, too. And this will work, up to a certain size and if you get good enough people in an organization, centralized authority will work and work better than any other organization, if you have the proper people, both experience, knowledgable, intelligent, and with the same objectives--it will work better than any other organization, just like a dictatorship is the most efficient of all organization so long as it's headed in the right direction. But when a organization gets so big, not all of it can be directed from the top. The more you centralize an organization, the more you cut down the initiative of the subordinates, and eventually it ends up with the top people doing all the thinking and all the ordering, and the lower people, junior people carrying out orders, without any authority themselves to initiate anything in carrying it through. That means you've got a lot fewer people working on the problem than you should have, when you centralize things. And centralization always comes a cropper eventually. Usually when you run out of people that started it.

Now, a dictatorship is usually efficient when it first starts. For three or four years a dictatorship is very efficient. And then people get in power, they like power, and I don't mean just the head man but the people who surround him--they like the prerogatives of power and they like more of it, and they get corrupted by power, as the old saying goes. They may become yes men, because the dictator first likes to have people oppose him, he wants to do the right thing for his government, but after a while, he gets a little irritated at people always opposing him, and so he makes a decree, and pretty soon people get the word and they don't oppose him so very much because he controls the destiny of the individuals, and those individuals want a very good destiny. So they say yes, and they give him what they think he wants. And at that time he doesn't have knowledge of what is going on below because he doesn't get the exact knowledge, he only gets what people want him to hear. So he loses contact with reality. Then he gets arbitrary and he starts to think, and the whole top of the organization starts to think that they have all the answers, that nobody else really knows anything, and they are destined to be--that they are endowed with super-knowledge.

Q: A sense of infallibility.

Burke: They're infallible, this is right. If they're not infallible they can at least make their decisions stick. And they can, for a while, until there's a general revulsion against that sort of stuff.

Now, centralization of the services is not quite that serious, but it has the same tendency, that if you centralize the services into one big service, with so many different facets, that people lose their knowledge of the individual facets, and they--and you end up with too much emphasis on one aspect of war and not enough emphasis on all **the aspects** of war. You're bound to make mistakes. In other words, you don't have the checks and balances that you would have if you had independent services. Now, there's such a thing as being too independent, too. There's got to be a compromise. You've got to reach a happy medium where people take independent action, but in coordination with other people who are working within the same policy that you're working in. Somebody knows, where somebody lays down a policy, the top people lay down policy--but the ways of accomplishing that policy are different in different areas of work.

This same thing happens in a company. It's what happens with conglomerates. Everybody thought that conglomerates were the answer to things, but the conglomerate didn't work except when they left the authority in the elements they'd assembled--decentralized it. Then those conglomerates worked, but those that didn't do that never had enough management capability to manage directly from the top. They couldn't do it. It's worse in the government because organizations are much bigger.

So I opposed this thing from the beginning, but it

didn't do very much good, although the President in re-organizing only did one thing that was seriously harmful to the Navy, and that was, he took command away from the Chief of Naval Operations and put the command in the Joint Chiefs of Staff.

Tape 2

Q: Admiral, why did the President insist on taking command of the Fleets away from CNO in this reorganization?

Burke: Well, primarily this was because of his Army background and because neither the Army nor the Air Force Chiefs of Staff commanded their forces, and he wanted to make all the services alike, so he cut the command of the Navy out from under the Chief of Naval Operations and made him have the same authority as the Chief of Staff of the Army.

Q: Now, he heard you out on this?

Burke: Oh yes. Oh yes, I had plenty of opportunity to express my views, which I did on many occasions. And he was unhappy with my testimony before Congress, and I sometimes got called by him on what I said before Congress, but they were the same things I said before to him. So I felt I should tell what I actually thought. If they asked me, I had to. And he understood that. He didn't like it but he understood it.

Q: Did you have the backing of the Secretary of the Navy in the position you took?

Burke: Oh yes.

Q: What about Secretary of Defense?

Burke: The Secretary of Defense was not very strong either way. This increased the authority of the Secretary of Defense and they naturally liked it, because every individual feels if he's good (and they were all good)--feels, "If only I could make those decisions, they would be better."

Well, the trouble was, as it turned out, that he didn't have time to make all those decisions. And I don't think they were better. Maybe it's all right. Any organization can be run, doesn't matter what it is, if you have the right people to run it. But you can never get enough right people to run it smoothly as it should be run, and you'd better get an organization that will run with a few good people, a small organization, and that you can determine who is doing a good job and who isn't. In other words, you have alternatives.

Q: Now, you had an opportunity to serve for a couple of years longer under this change. Did you feel that it truly detracted from the role of the CNO?

Burke: Yes, it did. It did, because for example in Quemoy and Matsu, and Lebanon both, I could give direct orders to the Fleet very fast. And did. Then I went down and explained it to the Chiefs, and they I think always agreed that I'd done the right thing.

Q: In effect it was a fait accompli anyhow.

Burke: It was a fait accompli, and I could explain it to them. But they all knew about it just as soon as it happened, so that I didn't catch anybody by surprise. After that, I went through the procedure of going down and explaining the thing in detail to the Joint Chiefs of Staff, and because they were responsible and jointly they wanted to make sure that they were not doing the wrong thing. Before that, if I did the wrong thing, I was responsible, not them, and it was my neck in the noose, and they didn't have to be so careful. But later they had to check and be very careful. Well, it meant that it took a long, long time to get things done, and lots of times, there was just a long discussion on what I thought was a very minute point not worth the discussion.

Q: Can you give an illustration of this delay which the

new setup--

Burke: --oh, I can't remember a specific incident, but I remember in general--there was nothing that I remember--- well, the Bay of Pigs, of course, but that was not a Joint Chiefs of Staff matter anyway, so that wasn't really--

Then, too, because we had all been Chiefs under the old system, it didn't change very much. I could send out, did send out to the Fleet commanders thereafter dispatches when I wanted them to do something and say, "I intend to take up with the Joint Chiefs of Staff the following, these orders," and they could prepare for them, and they knew what I would want to do and usually I could get it through the Joint Chiefs of Staff. But it wasn't quite as serious as later on it turned out to be when there were new people.

I don't think it really hampered me very much as an individual. It has since then. It's always harder to run things by committee than it is directly. At the same time there are some advantages to a committee, too.

Q: This was a happy choice you made in anticipatory orders to commanders of the Fleet.

Burke: Of course, I usually did that anyway. If I was thinking I might do something, if there was more than a 50 or 60 percent chance of doing it, I would give them the dope as soon as I could so that they could prepare for it, and they sometimes came in and said, "Don't do it that way, let's do it some other way."

Q: You did welcome the reaction from them.

Burke: Yes.

Q: Several component parts of the Navy were in jeopardy, as I understand it, during this reorganization development in '58, one of them being the status of the Marine Corps.

Burke: Yes. Many Army officers felt that the Marine Corps was the Navy's Army, and that they should have just one Army and the Marine Corps should not be in existence.

Q: In spite of the marvelous record in World War II in the Pacific?

Burke: Yes, but theoretically they still--it doesn't matter about the record or the individuals, theoretically it looked like they ought to have just one Army, and they said that if the Marines had been in the Army they would have done just as well as they did with the Navy. Well, of course, this is not true, because they're trained differently. They're trained for amphibious warfare. They're trained for small unit warfare, a lot of other things, and also they were in competition with the Army and a little competition is good, too. The Marines had to do better because they always have done better and they intend to keep it that way.

Q: And being small, exclusive--

Burke: It was an exclusive elitist group, yes. So that-- although it was a difficult time, the Marines were not in nearly as much danger of losing their identity then as they were under President Truman. They came close under President Truman. But we could point to the law, and all the arguments that we'd gone through before, and we had more support on the Hill for a Marine Corps than we did under President Truman, so that battle, although it was serious, we felt we could win that.

Q: What was the President's attitude toward the Marine Corps?

Burke: He never made a statement that the Marine Corps should be part of the Army. I never heard him. I don't think he ever did. I think he kept his hands off of that pretty much. I think he didn't make the mistake that President Truman did, but I think he would have not been unhappy either way. I don't think he had a strong point of view on that.

Now, we also had trouble with our aviation, too.

Q: In '58?

Burke: Yes. They wanted to cut our carriers, both the other services did, the Air Froce more than the Army, but still they both wanted to make drastic cuts. This was a question of money and primarily--carriers cost money, airplanes cost money, and we proved, first by our history, what we had been able to accomplish that nobody else could have accomplished, and we also proved to Congress that the only way we could do many jobs was with mobile air, carry our air bases with us--that the Air Force simply could not do many of the jobs with land-based air. Just as right now in this particular situation in Vietnam, they could not possibly have done that job with just land-based air. They need naval air, naval air is stretched very thin at the moment. But over and over again, the Air Force felt that we were duplicating their mission, that there was only one group that should be responsible for aircraft and that should be them. Well, this is not true. Actually I think that it would be much better if the Army had more of its own air, although it has a great deal more now than it did then, but they have to have a pretty sizeable air force and the Navy has to have a pretty sizeable air detachment too, for them to keep alive, and for them to fulfill the missions of the United States, not just the missions of their service.

But what we lost in '58 was not so much the loss in the individual services as control of the individual services--control of the departments shifted from the Secretaries of Navy, Army and Air Force to the Secretary of Defense, and from the Chiefs of Staff of the various services to the Joint Chiefs of Staff, so that now all problems, all important tactical and strategic problems are settled by committee or by the Secretary of Defense, instead of by the people who certainly should be more competent than the people in the other services.

Q: There was a very great downgrading then of the individual Secretaries.

Burke: Yes, and more centralization in the Department of Defense. And I don't think that's improved any of the services at all.

Q: Admiral, I am aware of the attitude of the Navy prior to that time, the Secretary of the Navy, his importance in the Navy structure--was this downgraded in the eyes of the Navy as a whole as a result of this?

Burke: Oh yes. He couldn't make decisions any more, the

Secretary of the Navy had to go to the Secretary of Defense to make any important decisions, so it downgraded the Secretary of the Navy more than anybody else, probably. He was taken off the Cabinet level and put down, just taken off, so he was no longer an important position in the hierarchy in government. That meant that civilians did not want that job if they could get a more important job, and any Cabinet job was more important than Secretary of one of the services. And I think this has shown--I think even currently right now, it's difficult to get a Secretary of a service, an excellent man. They don't want to serve.

Also, we had at that time, I was very fortunate in my Secretaries of the Navy, they were all good people, but Mr. Franke was especially good at that time. I don't know whether it was Gates--I guess it was Gates was Secretary of the Navy at that time and Gates was very good, too. They worked with the Navy. There's need for a civilian Secretary as an interface between the military and the rest of the civilian government. There's a great need for that. It the Secretary and the Chief of service get along well together, then there can be discussions and arguments, differences of opinion-- and the relationship with the rest of the government is much smoother than if they just had the military there by themselves. It's a very important position.

The Secretary of the Navy is now a subordinate of the Secretary of Defense. He doesn't have the authority to go to the President if he differs with the Secretary of Defense. The Chiefs still do. But it's downgraded no end.

Q: You told me the other day about the first meeting with President Eisenhower, then president of Columbia University, and the briefing you gave him on naval aviation and the use of carriers, and you said at that time that he had not had any real knowledge of the actual use of carriers, and you had attempted to indoctrinate him from the Navy point of view and you thought you'd been successful, but you discovered later that you weren't quite as successful as you thought you had been. Were you referring to this period in 1958 when the carriers were cut?

Burke: Yes. That and--after a demonstration of what we could do, which he appreciated and understood very well, he couldn't take that lesson in a general way. He applied it very specifically to that particular problem. The mobility of carriers was something that he didn't--he never did quite hoist aboard all the advantages it gave to a nation.

Q: Well, with his overriding responsibilities as President, was it the financial aspect which entered into the picture and overruled the other?

Burke: No. I don't think it was ever that clear. Of course, finances always entered into most every problem, but I don't think it was--it wasn't either/or. It was just a question of lack of understanding of the full capabilities of naval air. He'd go aboard ship, and he'd be very impressed with what we could do, but he didn't apply it to enough situations, to another situation. Still he was as good as--no man can know everything, and he was a very good President. He was understanding to a pretty good extent. Matter of fact I don't see how--it takes a man of great experience to be a good President, and experience in more than just in politics, I think.

Q: And in this dangerous world in which we live, a knowledge of military capabilities seems to be an awfully good and necessary background. How does a non-military man who's never been exposed to that acquire it in a brief period of time when he becomes President?

Burke: I don't think he does, and I think it'll be a long time now, with the attitude of the country the way it is, before they give much emphasis, much weight to a man's military experience in selecting a President. I think rather they would tend not to have a military man, a man with much military experience, as President. It's important, but it's also important that he knows a great deal about economics, world economics and political matters, too. It's a job in which I supposed nobody is really qualified, until after he's been President for a while.

Q: Would you comment on the DEW line that was built and our Early Warning System in the days when early warning was something that counted in terms of intercontinental ballistic missiles?

Burke: Well, this thing really started with bombers. Of course, it was impossible initially to find out, to know for sure that Russian bombers had taken off for an attack upon the United States, and the only way you could tell-- we didn't have enough intelligence. There was no way of getting intelligence in those days. So the only way you could do it was to put radars as far forward as possible, over the flight paths that they probably would use. This was the first of the DEW Lines. I think they had a few radars up in Canada, and this was when we first became involved because one of the best bomber routes was across the Northern Atlantic, and we had to put ships out with radar to detect possible bombers. This was a very heavy thing because ships just stayed there, it was boring duty and, of course, nothing happened.

Then as they got missiles, it became more important because the time, the--instead of the hours warning you had with bombers, you had minutes, in missiles. So we had to get them as close to the enemy as possible. Until they decided after great controversy to build--I think it was three big radar, tremendous radar stations--but before that they built a lot of radar stations up in northern Canada, clear across Canada, and we put radars aboard ships that were specially used for high altitude long range work, for just warning radars to fill the gaps that could not be filled by land-based radar. This cost a tremendous amount of money, the whole works.

Then as radars became bigger and more effective, they decided to put one radar in northern Scotland, I think it was, one in Newfoundland and one in Alaska, then they put one in Turkey, to pick up Soviet missiles as soon as we possibly could. These radars were tremendous fixed array systems that cost in the hundreds of millions of dollars total. Even then, those radars--they took the most likely flight paths, but they didn't fill all the gaps. There were gaps in between what those radars covered.

Q: And the locations were known to the enemy?

Burke: The locations were exactly known to the enemy, and

one of the first things they would do, of course, would be to knock out the radars, which in itself would have been an early warning. But still the timing--they could do that and you'd never know for sure if it was intentional, you'd be pretty sure.

But in any case, this was a very expensive operation, which lasted only a few years, 10 or 15 years. Now DEW Line is obsolete and I doubt if it's manned. Parts of it are manned, I'm sure now.

Q: The President was interested in this whole thing and didn't demur at the cost?

Burke: Oh yes, he demurred at the cost all right, and he tried to cut the cost all the time and did. So he got it as cheap as possible, but it was very difficult to get the equipment that would work under those very severe conditions, or the men who would operate the equipment under such conditions. But he supported it in general. He knew it was necessary.

Q: How did you feel about it?

Burke: Well, I felt that we didn't have to have complete coverage, that to get anything from 90 percent coverage to 100 percent coverage takes a lot of money, a lot more effort. This is true in almost any type of equipment or operation. Sometimes it takes as much effort to get the last 10 percent effectiveness as it does to get the first 90 percent effectiveness. This is true with the DEW Line. Air Force wanted to make certain that no one missile could come over the United States without them knowing about it. That cost a tremendous amount of money, whereas if you were sure that you could pick up three out of ten missiles, you'd have pretty good warning, because they wouldn't shoot just one missile over one flight path where you didn't have a radar station, didn't have a method of detecting it, and this was particularly true if the enemy didn't know exactly your capabilities. They'd always be taking a chance. So I felt that we were spending more money than necessary. But I lost on that, and as it turned out we never used it at all. But still some method of detection was necessary at that time.

Q: In your time as CNO there was a NATO military mission, was there not?

Burke: Yes.

Q: What role did you play in supervising the attitude of the US member of that mission?

Burke: Well, of course all the services briefed the people who were in NATO. Most of the NATO people were Army people, because of US SAC Eur, but US SAC Eur and--I mean SAC Eur was a Supreme allied Commander but he was the same man as US CINC Eur. In other words, Commander of U.S. Forces Europe. Same thing was true with SAC Lant and US CINC Lant. It was the same individual. So there we had to be very sure those commanders understood exactly what the US position was and what he should do with the US forces, and at the same time be fair with NATO and make sure that he actually operated as a Supreme Allied Commander. But in those days, too, the United States had the most influence in NATO councils because we were the ones that had the power. We were the ones that had the equipment and the people, and so what we wanted usually was what happened, so you had to be very careful to make sure that you didn't express something that wasn't really good for SAC Eur or for NATO.

Now, they had a NATO standing group in Washington, on which we had a member, a Navy member. Sometimes Navy, sometimes Army but during my time it was Navy. That man had to be very familiar with the US position, not only just Navy position but the other services' positions and the differences between them, and what the United States position was. He could never violate the United States position, but he had to know the background of how that United States position was arrived at.

So we spent a great deal of time briefing these people.

Q: He also had to be something of a diplomat, didn't he, dealing with the French especially.

Burke: Well, the French. Surprisingly enough, we've always had very good relationships with the French, even when France withdrew from NATO, that is, the Navy did. Naval operations continued, just about as much as they did before France withdrew, but they were not under the name of NATO. Cooperation was pretty good, and a good many people in the French military services didn't approve of de Gaulle's withdrawing from NATO. So they would help us as much as they could within the limits of their orders.

Q: This was something particularly within the cognizance of President Eisenhower. Did he play any role with the military mission?

Burke: Not directly, but he was very careful. Of course, NATO was always near to his heart, and he stressed NATO all the time. I'm sure that he made sure that good people were assigned and that those people were adequately briefed, but he himself I don't think met with them very often. Once in a while.

Q: The US member of the standing group did confer with the President, but ordinarily you were the one who had to bear that responsibility?

Burke: Yes. But NATO relationships were very good while we were there. There were differences--our allies never contributed as much as we thought they should, and they were always demanding more than they could reasonably expect. And they expected more of the United States than we were willing to give. But we gave a lot more than I think any other nation has ever given to its allies before.

Q: Were they trading on our very great interest in NATO and initial efforts setting it up, trading on this when they asked so much?

Burke: Somewhat. Of course, any nation, any national wants to do the best he can for his particular nation, and if he can get a combine to carry part of that nation's load, more of the common load, if his nation can carry less of the common load, then it's economic advantage, military advantage, lots of advantages. All nations try that. The Germans, we disarmed them--the Germans had lost the war. They didn't feel like they could ask their people to carry that kind of a load. Lots of our allies didn't want the Germans re-armed very much, and before they came into NATO, in the discussions when they did come into NATO, there were quite a few nations, mostly French but also the British, who were fearful of the Germans, of re-arming Germany. Germany felt, well, as long as they don't want us to re-arm, why should we? Let them carry it. And they made very great economic advances because they didn't have the military expenditures. Same thing was true in Japan.

But on the other hand, we would like to have our allies carry a lot more load and ease our load, and perhaps if we could do it we probably would do it but they just won't do it.

Q: What role did you play in the negotiations for the Spanish bases and the submarine base in Scotland? In the fifties-- this happened during your regime.

Burke: Yes. Well, first there was the selection of the bases, where we would have them. First the political climate had to be proper. It had to be some nation that we could depend upon a great deal. Stability in the nation. Then it had to have good operating conditions. So we searched all over. We determined that northern Scotland was the best place for a base, and then we ought to have a base for the Mediterranean. If we put it inside the Mediterranean, we could either put it in Spain or Italy or France, and we-- Malta looked to have great advantages, and Malta would have been pretty good, but Malta was extremely unstable even then, although the facilities there were--

Q: Mintoff was in the ascendancy, was he?

Burke: Yes. Mintoff was on the horizon. I don't think he was in the ascendancy then. But if we put the base in the Med, there were lots of disadvantages in going through the Straits of Gibraltar and possibly the base could be destroyed a little more easily. So we decided to try outside the Mediterranean but close to the Straits of Gibraltar. So this is how we chose one at Rota.

Then by that time I had extremely close relationships with all the chiefs of the other navies. I'd worked on this. I'm still very good friends with many of the Chiefs, and I go to see them and they come to see me, still years later.

Q: How did you achieve that initially?

Burke: Having them come over, talking over their problems and our problems, and see what we had in common and then how we could help each other, but mostly to make sure that you learned to trust one another, to find out whether they're really trustworthy or not, and most of them were. Of course, some of them had limited--they were themselves trustworthy, but you couldn't trust what their governments might do in the future.

But we got the help of the Navy people in the country for the support of these bases--Mountbatten did an awful lot to get our base in Scotland, and Arfe thusa I think was the Spanish Chief of Naval Operations, chief of the naval staff, helped us in Rota. But we had to build Rota. They gave us a lot of advantages, privileges in Rota that they normally wouldn't have done. They didn't do it with the Air Force, but they gave us a lot of authority.

Q: Because of the relationship Navy-wise?

Burke: Yes. I think so. But those bases took a very long time, much longer than we thought. It just took a long time to get things through the parliaments, get it all wrapped up.

Q: I would judge that maybe John Lodge was the right person in Spain at that time to help with this problem.

Burke: Was John Lodge there? Yes, he was. He was extremely good. At that time, he was promoted to captain in the naval reserve, and I got him a placque, some sort of citation, as Captain-Ambassador. The reason for that is that--

Q: Columbus was a captain something or other.

Burke: Yes, and the Spanish use that system a lot. They have captain generals and a lot of peculiar titles in their military.

Interview with Admiral Arleigh Burke   December 12, 1972
by John T. Mason, Jr.   Washington, D. C.

Q: Admiral it's good to see you this morning. I'm looking forward to a continuation of your discussion of your years as Chief of Naval Operations. When we broke off, you were dealing with the Spanish base for Polaris submarines, Rota, and I think perhaps you want to say more about that.

Admiral Burke: Well, I think we did say something about the reason why it was put in the Atlantic rather than in the Mediterranean, but there is a little more to it.

One of the things that's most important in establishing a base in a foreign country is the stability of the country, how long is that country going to be our ally, how long is it going to support it? Because international relations, although it seems like it changes very slowly, actually it changes quite fast. That is exemplified by the fact that our two great enemies in World War II were very shortly after World War II our best supporters, best allies. This, of course, is one thing that you have to be very careful of. We had some good allies at that time in the Mediterranean, Turkey, Greece, Italy, France. Spain was not in NATO and not really an ally of ours. So before we decided on which country we would like to go in, we made an analysis of the stability of those countries, and in spite of the fact that at that time all the countries were probably better, more friendly towards the United States than Spain, this was their government and the view of their government, and in Spain the support of Americans went down through all the people. In all the other countries there were dissident groups as has been proven since that time. So we decided that our best bet for the long term support was Spain rather for example France, where there were bases--we could have obtained bases perhaps on both the Mediterranean and the Atlantic.

The Rota base, another factor about it is that it cost very much. It cost a great deal. They had to build a breakwater, a tremendous breakwater, and we analyzed the building of breakwaters, cost of breakwaters. The Navy's had quite a bit of experience in building breakwaters--for example, the one in Long Beach, California cost us perhaps twice as much, not Navy money but California money. It cost over twice as much as our original estimate and took twice as many rocks, stones. And the breakwater didn't always work very well. In heavy storms the breakwater would be broached now and then and had to be repaired at great expense.

We had a civil engineer, Chief of the Bureau of Yards

and Docks, I've forgotten his name now, big tall lad, and he said, "Well, the reason is the waves aren't broken up early enough in the game, particularly down at sea bottom where the real strength is, as the shelf shallows and comes nearer to the breakwater." So he said that if we put in tetrahedons, big concrete ones, not just rocks, it would break the wave action up and probably work very well. He said we could control the sea force a little bit more, maybe.

Q: Was any of this knowledge a carry-over from Normandy, the landings?

Burke: I'm sure it was, but I don't know that. I'm sure that it was. The Normandy landings, they didn't build breakwaters. What they did was to build surface ports, barges, MULBERRY. Yes, they did build some breakwaters too, but they relied mostly upon breaking the surface action, which is all right for a while. But as it turned out this tetrahedon business has been very effective and Rota has been a good base.

I don't think tetrahedons for that purpose was invented then. I think it was invented before. But thank goodness the engineer from Bureau of Yards and Docks thought of that idea. This man now works for Sverdrup and Co. in St. Louis. He works with Jack Sverdrup who's an Army officer and one of the best engineers the Army ever had. I knew him in the Solomons and in the States.

Q: I suppose you had to endure a certain amount of flak in this country, didn't you, for making these arrangements with Spain?

Burke: Yes, there was some flak, but there always is. No matter what you do, if you have to go through Congress there will be some Congressmen who will oppose it, and this is not bad. This means you have to make sure you know what you're doing. But I'm sure there was quite a bit of flak, and I'm sure there was--the people who were opposed to Franco raised quite a bit of trouble. But I don't remember that it was too severe. I've forgotten about any incident then so it couldn't have been too bad.

Q: Was there any concern on the part of the Spanish government, pollution of the waters, anything of that sort, with Polaris submarines?

Burke: No. You mean nuclear pollution? No. No, the only one by that time concerned about nuclear submarines polluting their harbors was Japan, and that was purely political because they really knew better but it was a good handle and a good argument, and even the Japanese proved to their satisfaction that no American submarine had ever polluted the harbor, except in one instance a very minor amount and then that could have been an error in the instruments.

Q: I remember Don Griffin telling me about the Seventh Fleet and the precautions he had to take in order to convince these people. Chiang Kai-chek I think was one who showed some concern about it.

Burke: He showed some concern because he was reading Japanese papers. But he came around pretty well. Chiang Kai-chek at that time was a very reasonable man.

Q: So the Rota base worked out well enough.

Burke: Yes. The one thing we had most difficulty with on the Rota base was, who commands it? Who runs the base? And this is one of the things that's most important, because if a foreign country can have the decision power or even great influence over the military activities that you want to conduct on your base, or determine--what you shall and shall not do, it's very likely that in a time of crisis, they will make a decision to go farther than they've ever gone before and you might not be able to move your forces, or if you did move them you would move them against force of your host country. This is why I objected to establishing such an extensive base in Okinawa, but they established it anyway. But Okinawa did have that trouble, and it's now a secondary and perhaps a useless base unless Japan itself decides to say they're in trouble and then they will want it back in a hurry, but you can never depend on a base, the use of a base in which a foreign nation has control.

Now, naturally we established Rota in Spain. This was in Spain's domain. That is, Spain and no other country wants to give up control of part of their territory. But they recognized that if we had to use that base, we had to be able to depend on the use of that base under any circumstances, so finally we were able to iron this out. They understood that.

Q: We paid a fair price financially for it.

Burke: We paid a tremendous price financially for it, and we also made arrangements for housing not only for Americans but for Spaniards, and we made arrangements some time in the future--I think it's a specific time in the future-- that Spanish military people would command the base. But they would not command American forces. They would not try to dictate, would have no authority to dictate what American forces would do, except that we would obey Spanish laws and normal things and they wouldn't interfere with our military operations. This was the Status of Forces agreement that we had so much difficulty with after World War II in all countries. What jurisdiction do we maintain over our own people? What jurisdiction does the foreign host nation maintain?

Q: I suppose there was some wisdom gleaned from the Guantanamo situation which was a carry-over and help in negotiating with Spain?

Burke: Well, I don't know who initially, dictated or developed the Guantanamo Agreement, but the Guantanamo Agreement was good for the United States. In fact, the agreement with Cuba in regard to Guantanamo status was very much like the agreement with Panama in regard to the Panama Canal, that we had the right of sovereignty for a 99 year lease and we paid Cuba so much per year in gold for many years but finally in just ordinary money. But we paid in gold after we'd gone off the gold standard. That was a very good agreement. We still have the right, by the agreement, to use that base as we see fit, so long as we don't violate Cuban territory.

Q: What about Holy Loch, Scotland?

Burke: Holy Loch is a little different. The British were very reluctant to have us establish a base in Britain any place.

Q: Why?

Burke: Nuclear things, that was one part. Mostly--that was a minor issue--mostly a lot of Americans in an area. It would be a targeted place for the enemy, so that it would require them, if they permitted us to establish a base there, it would require them to support us in the use of that base, and they might get tied into a future action of the United States which Britain didn't want to get tied into. Those are all good reasons.

On the other hand, we were allies, we were protecting Britain, Britain should contribute something. All they had to contribute to that was a harbor/ a space to overhaul ships, no facilities, no big facilities, and we finally worked out an agreement which was that we would use tenders instead of establishing a big group ashore, and that we would not--we would keep our submarines on the surface till we got a certain distance from Holy Loch, so that we would not use Holy Loch as a launching area; that we would not try to take over the local towns, wherever they were. They wanted to choose the area--this is all right, we said, fine, this is what we'd like to have in the base. I've forgotten what all the things were, but they were probably specifics.

They picked Holy Loch in essence and we accepted it, although we inspected it very carefully, and Holy Loch as it turned out is a very good base.

Q: Had they used it in any way as a base?

Burke: Yes. I don't think there's any port in England that hasn't been used as a base some time or other, but not very much. It's not like Scapa Flow or Portsmouth, because it's not close to the scene of action.

Q: It wasn't prominent in World War II.

Burke: No, it wasn't because it was on the wrong side of Scotland. They did use it in World War II as a base for some of their convoy escorts, but it wasn't extensively used. But that was a very good choice and it turned out very well. Of course, after we established the tenders over there, then the British populace liked our people, whom they thought they would not like, so we were very careful to send good solid people and no trouble makers, I mean no agitators and people who would appreciate what the British attitudes were. We gave them a good course of instruction before they went over, and our people did a magnificent job and the British liked them very much.

Q: The Polaris crews in themselves are superior men,

aren't they?

Burke: Well, they are, because they live very closely together and they have to be selected psychologically in order to live that locsely together without antagonizing other people. But mostly it was education, instruction, and they did a very good job. Later the British inhabitants around Holy Loch wanted more and more Americans to come over there. They liked us. They liked the dollars. They liked the things that Americans did. I think it's still probably true. I don't know that now.

Q: I've heard that the need for Holy Loch and Rota has lessened now, and there has been some discussion perhaps of not using these bases in the future?

Burke: There was never an absolute need for Holy Loch or Rota. There never was. We based Polaris building program on not having to use any foreign bases whatever. But what those bases did do was that they permitted more time on station and less time in transit to the station, if they had to transit from the US to their stations there would be a lot more time that they were not on station with the same number of submarines.

Q: And that reason has not lessened?

Burke: Yes, it has lessened because the missiles are much

longer range now, and so the stations that they have to go to are not nearly as far away from the United States, not necessarily as far away from the United States as they had to be in those days. 1500--originally, a 1200 mile missile, you have to be fairly close to the coastline of your target.

Q: Ambassador Hill told me recently that he was involved in the re-negotiation of the Spanish base. Have we had to renegotiate Holy Loch?

Burke: I don't know. I don't think so. I think the agreement has to be extended periodically. I'm sure it's not an indeterminate agreement. But I don't know whether there's any renegotiation there.

One of the things we gave the British, one of the reasons why the British were so helpful, was that we helped them a great deal in the development of their own Polaris submarines. This was Mountbatten's request (which I tried to dissuade him,) for Britain going into Polaris type submarines, but he wanted to do it and he wanted to do it very badly.

Q: For prestige?

Burke: Presitige primarily, but not altogether. You see,

a nation--the influence that a nation has on other nations, or influence in the trend of future events, is dependent upon the power of the nation, and it's not just actual power of a nation because nobody really knows that, but it depends upon what other nations think the power of the nation is, and that power includes, of course, political, military, economic, psychological, all the other kinds of power. The Soviets, of course, have used propaganda to increase our ideas of what Soviet power is a great deal, and sometimes they have been able to out-maneuver us because we thought, like the missile crisis, we thought, some people thought that they had a great deal more power than they actually had. This is, of course, one of the major reasons why they will not permit inspection.

So Britain, the British know the use of power in international relations probably better than any other nation. They've been very skillful at that for a couple of hundred years. And so what they needed was nuclear delivery capability. They needed to belong to the nuclear club, and they needed to belong to the nuclear club no fooling without just a facade which France and China had at the beginning. They wanted to make sure that their capability would really work.

Well, that meant that either they had to adopt our systems pretty thoroughly, completely, or they had to go through a very expensive development to develop what we had already developed. And what I suggested to Mountbatten, to Dickie Mountbatten, was, first not to go into nuclear power at all, for delivery capability, because they couldn't afford any significant delivery capability, anything that would really change the outcome of a war that was once started, but if he did, if Britain did insist on having such a delivery capability, then it would be a lot cheaper for Britain to just buy American Polaris submarines at cost and they'd save a tremendous amount. They'd have had to tool up and all the other things for just a very few submarines. At that time I think initially Mountbatten thought that perhaps they would have as many as ten, Polaris submarines, but he never thought of more than ten. As it turned out, I think they settled for four or five.

Did this require amendment to our National Defense Act?

Burke: No. No, because we had already had an amendment, Britain being the most favored nation, whic, of course, is the main reason why France was upset always, they never trusted the United States and Britain when they talked to one another because France was not part of the nuclear club, and this caused de Gaulle and all Frenchmen a great deal of difficulty. And I think we were in error on that. But anyway since World War II Britain has this preferred position, and you will even now in conferences or conversations with the British, they will bring up that extra close relationship of the United States and Britain. Now, the extra close relationship means different things to British people than it means to us, but--they took advantage of that. This is one of the reasons that so many British people did not want to go into the Common Market.

But Dickie Mountbatten, who exemplified the glory of Great Britain, the power of Great Britain--last Viceroy of India--he was sent there to sell the British Empire and get the best deal he could get, but get rid of it, get rid of India. He voted to get rid of India no matter what, no matter what he had to do, but he got the best deal he could get--which he did and he did very well. Except in separating India and Pakistan.

Well, anyway, he wanted Britain to remain as powerful as it possibly could. He recognized that Britain would have a great deal of trouble in having real power, but if he couldn't have real power, then he wanted to have the trappings of power, some power, and some power is very valuable.

For example, if a nation has even a very small nuclear delivery capability, it can have an influence totally out of proportion to the actual military strength of that nuclear capability, because they can mess things up, they can mess relations up, they can get tough and say, "If you don't do what I want you to do, what we want to do, then we're going to go out on our own and we will wreck your plans by taking independent action."

This, of course, de Gaulle was an expert in, later he did just that. But I told Dickie down in Key West when he came over and we went down there to go through a flock of ships, showing some of our stuff, I told Dickie, "We will help you, but we think you should change your mind. I think you should change your mind. But if you don't, we will help you on your Polaris. We will do everything we can, if we can check the people you send over here, we will put your people directly into our schools--we're going to check them out individually. We will control very carefully the top secret information which we give to them, but we will give you all the dope you need, all the information you need and really all that you need so that you can operate these submarines and build them, design them, so that they'll be capable submarines."

Well, this was going pretty far, for us. But there's no use having a half-hearted ally. It's better to have no allies than a dissatisfied ally or an unhappy ally, or more than that, an untrusting ally, and if you want to get trust, you have to make sure that the man you're talking to is first trustworthy, and then second if he is you have to give him trust. He's not going to have confidence in you if you don't have confidence in him. That doesn't mean that you have confidence in anybody. But our willingness to help Britain in her nuclear capability was a tremendous factor, and perhaps--I'm sure it was the major factor in their willingness to do what they did in regard to Holy Loch and other support.

Q: How did the President feel about all of this?

Burke: Oh, the President is a very understanding man, and he knew more about national power and the uses of national power than I thought he did. He really knew that. Since we've both gotten out of office, I have come to appreciate his finesse, his knowledge of what it takes to deal with nations. He recognized the need for power of a nation and the need not to over-use power. Now, this--our strategy, and perhaps I got this from him, I wouldn't be at all surprised, it's hard to tell who you learn things from--but our methods of operation have to be completely different from that of the Soviets. The Soviets can be devious, they can lie, they can pretend that they have things that they do not have, or they can pretend equally that they do not have things, that they are not doing things that they actually are doing, because of their form of government and their tight security operations, their whole method of operation.

Q: They're not burdened with freedom of the press.

Burke: They're not burdened with freedom of the press. But freedom of the press isn't all of it. It's a good indication of the rest of it. The United States has got to really have power. We can't kid anybody, because somebody-- It would leak out very fast; in our own internal, internal arguments in Congress, a foreign nation can get a very accurate measure of our real power, just from reading the CONGRESSIONAL RECORD even after the testimony has been censored. So we have to have real power. We have to have the skill and the ability to use it, and they have to know that, too. That is the only thing that they need have very much doubt about--how skillful are we, how willing, what attitudes will we adopt?

And, of course, this is the very reason why the Germans twice misread the intentions of the United States. We didn't have those intentions but they misread what we would probably do. Twice they thought we were a decadent people and twice they thought that there was so much opposition in this country to having a war at all that they estimated that we would not come in, in both World War I and World War II, and they did things, they went too far, and we did go into war, and both times they were very much surprised.

The same thing is happening right now in this Vietnam situation, where the Communists thought that Mr. McGovern had a tremendous following in this country and that the majority of the people were opposed to what the government of the United States was then doing, and they were completely wrong.

Q: It's understandable because we had doubts ourselves.

Burke: Oh yes, Mr. McGovern thought so, too. Yes, this is right. But many wars have been started, as has been pointed out many times, because a nation that later turned the balance didn't make its intentions clear that it was going to do that, that it was going to take action, early enough. Both World War I and World War II could have been avoided if not only the United States but other nations had been willing initially to state that they would fight rather than do it. Now, sadly enough, at the time that that would have been possible, they probably weren't sure they would fight. But certainly we did not make it clear to Italy and to Germany before World War II that we might go in.

Q: Admiral, since you were on the subject of submarines,

it was natural to get into the various expeditions to the Arctic that were conducted during your regime, and there were a number, climaxed, of course, with the NAUTILUS. Do you want to tell us about the reasons for these scientific expeditions, focus on that?

Burke: Well, yes. We know even now very little about the Arctic. We didn't know the depth of the water. We didn't know how deep ice goes down from the icebergs, whether it's even or not. We didn't know about currents in the Arctic or winds, and we didn't know what the thickness of the ice was. We knew practically nothing about the Arctic. The Arctic was one of the last areas of the world that had not been explored.

Now, there's another factor that is important in this, and it's a psychological factor, in addition. It has a great deal more importance than most people give it. That is, we climb mountains because the mountain is there. The Americans fortunately want to do things that nobody else has ever done. We want to be the first to do things. And when we lose that, we will have lost a great deal of energy and enthusiam and drive which makes people successful.

Q: That's part of the pioneering spirit, isn't it?

Burke: Yes. That's probably why most people, at least

one factor in why most people came to this country--why our ancestors came to this country in the first place.

So there was a good deal of that in it too--nobody has done this, let me do it. Well, what can the nation get out of it? We got as much as we could. There was quite a bit we didn't know that we should have known. So that's the reason why we did it.

Now, another factor, of course, that bothers me tremendously is, because we didn't know anything, we wanted to do a little probing. We didn't want to send a submarine from west to east or east to west across the Arctic and maybe not have it get there. So we did a lot of probing under the ice for short distances to see what was there, whether the thing could possibly be done.

Q: Every summer for about ten years.

Burke: Yes. As a matter of fact, even before then. When I was captain, rather executive office of a destroyer (new destroyer), we were sent up to the Arctic to see whether we could operate in cold weather under Arctic conditions. Actually we found the coldest weather off Maine--we operated there and that was horrible. Our ships weren't designed for cold weather.

Q: This was in the Atlantic entirely.

Burke: Yes. But we got all the ice, all the Arctic knowledge that we could get, Canadians and Americans, people who had studied ice and lived in the Arctic, knew the Arctic, even the lore we got, so that we weren't--at least we'd considered everything that we could find, and we did. Then the question was, should a submarine go from the Atlantic to the Pacific or the other way around, and why? Does it make any difference? And, of course, the difference was that the ports were closer on the Atlantic and it was a wider choice of courses of action.

Q: And the water was deeper.

Burke: The water was deeper. There were lots of minor reasons, but it all added up that we should go from west to east, which we did.

I must admit that it's very hard--I had some difficulty in getting this authorized, because we were jeopardizing to some extent, to an unknown extent really, the submarine and the people in it. We were jeopardizing our reputation, risking it, and the people--for results which might not be as important as we thought they would be.

Q: Who was reluctant to go along with it?

Burke: Everybody. Everybody.

Q: The Joint Chiefs, you mean?

Burke: Yes. They didn't see any purpose in it initially. And so--but the President was not very happy about it, either, because he would have to authorize it, such an unusual thing, or at least tacitly authorize it, permit it. He would have to know about it and if he knew about it and he didn't like it and he permitted it to go on anyway, it would end up as his responsibility.

Now, you don't want, Presidents certainly don't want to authorize an expedition which couldn't possibly have very much benefit and which has great risks to the people.

Q: The same thing as that expedition to the moon with no intention of returning--that he wouldn't agree to.

Burke: No, he wouldn't, and this was right. He was quite right. It ends up in the long run, in an argument like that where a man is doubtful, and he should be doubtful, that the man who is arguing for the thing, who's proposing it, has got to lay his own convictions on the table.

Q: That's what you did.

Burke: Sure. And he has to do this over and over again, not just on this--he has to do that over and over again, and every man does that. "I am sure this will work all right,

I am--I'd like to go on it myself if you'd permit it--"
"Oh no." "But it's going to turn out all right."

And it ends up, like most big decisions end up, not so much on factors of delicate accurate analysis of all the technical factors that go into an operation, but it ends up in the confidence that the top man has in the man who is suggesting it.

Q: The confidence that the President has in the CNO.

Burke: That's right, and the confidence that I had in our people. Same thing. It goes all the way down and all the way up.

This is what irritates a great many people who can't see why other people don't accept the logic of a course of action, and they don't accept the logic of a course of action because they don't know who's running the course of action, or they don't have confidence in who's running it. I don't mean that technical factors are wholly disregarded, of course they aren't, but basically it's faith. A man's got to have faith. He's got to have faith in people and he's got to know that faith, he's got to be convinced that that faith is well placed. This is true in any operation.

Q: Faith and a conviction that the results are worth the effort. And this is what you thought, the results were worth the effort. What was it you sought primarily, what sort of knowledge?

Burke: What we were seeking: two things. Would it be possible, was it possible for the Soviets for example, to operate in the Arctic in such a way as to jeopardize the security of the nation, our nation, without us knowing really anything about it, and without us knowing what countermeasures to take or having the ability to take countermeasures. In other words, it might be possible for them to take action, a surprise action which would put us way, way at a tremendous disadvantage, and we would be helpless.

The other one was, just the reverse: what could we do to enhance the probability of success in our operations? Would it be possible for example, to fire from the Arctic, without the Soviets--would it have great advantages? Was there some way we could get through this ice? Were there ways that would give us advantage? Would it give us good surveillance ability that we now didn't have, over the Russians? The stakes weren't very high but they were unknown stakes.

Q: These must have seemed good reasons to the President, who had to be concerned about our national security?

Burke: Well, they were. But still, you never know. The

possibilities are there, but the probability of a complete surprise move from a situation like that was not great. And it's a question of, how great is it? And nobody knows. Nobody knows now.

So you make an estimate. Is the risk worth the probable--is the probable payoff worth the risk? It's always a gamble.

Q: With these motives in mind, was this the reason for the extreme secrecy of the NAUTILUS operation, until it became a success?

Burke: Well, that was, of course, the major factor, but there were other factors, too. Since World War II, there has been a tendency in the United States to ballyhoo what you are going to do, and sometimes it wouldn't work. This happened over and over again, "We are great because we are going to do this," but they haven't done it. This can be-- this is not a good way to operate. You ought to do something and then if it's good you can announce, "I am really great because I did it," but not that, "I am really great because I am going to do it."

Now, we still have that tendency--but there was a great deal of that in it, too. We wanted to have a fait accompli, if we could do it we wanted to have done it before we announced it.

Then another thing is, we didn't know what the Soviet capability was and if we made a big ballyhoo about us going to the Arctic, it might have been very easy for them to have done something which would jeopardize or hazard our mission without us knowing anything about it. It was just as well they didn't know anything about it either. That's one unnecessary chance we didn't have to take.

Q: Upon the completion of the mission then we were able to make the announcement from the White House, were we not?

Burke: Yes. And that was very good. Now, President Eisenhower felt exactly the same way we did, all of us felt about that. He didn't want any preliminary announcements. Another thing, on this secrecy thing, you can carry that too far also. You can make it so secret it doesn't work. If you keep it secret from people who really ought to know about it to help support the project. And it's very difficult for Americans to keep a secret. They like to talk. All of us do.

I had a good example of that when I was captain of the USS MUGFORD. I was in Boston, and a seaman wanted leave. He wanted 30 days leave and he had the leave coming to him, but I wouldn't grant him the leave because we were about to sail for the West Coast, and after I'd refused it, why, his wife asked if she could see me. Sure. She came up and said, "Sir, we are not going to sail for the West Coast when you think we are."

"You don't know anything about this, little girl."

"Oh, yes I do."

I said, "No, you don't, you couldn't. I have instructions here, you don't know anything about it."

"Well, if you're so sure of that, will you grant my husband leave, up to 30 days, and up to the day before you sail?"

I said, "What are you going to do?"

She said, "We're going across country."

I said, "You can't get back here."

She said, "Then you've got him for AWOL. He won't be here. So you court martial him."

I said, "All right, if you're willing to do that, I'll do that."

You know, we didn't sail when we were scheduled. Why didn't we sail? Because that little girl's sister was working in the Navy Department and had told her, and she had the dope before I did, the skipper.

Well, this happens all the time. That wasn't an important thing. But Americans cannot keep secrets. So we were frightfully restricted, about the Bay of Pigs, where the data were so restricted that the people who were permitted to know were so few, that the operation perhaps could have been successful if more people had been able to study the operation and work on it and still keep it secret.

But Anderson who had command of the NAUTILUS then, Commander Anderson was an ideal man for that. He had the NAUTILUS--

Q: --then Calvert had it.

Burke: Calvert had it, and then Wilkinson. But they were all excellent people. They did a magnificent job. The technical people did a magnificent job too, excellent. They found a lot of very unusual things, that we thought were unusual then, about ice conditions, about the depth and thickness of ice and different composition of ice, the way ice drifts, the holes that are in the Arctic that you can come up, how to bore through ice. I wanted to go up there myself and I never was able to while I was on active duty, but I'm working with a man now, Shirtsinger, who is developing a cargo submarine which can carry oil primarily or any liquid, and this is a tremendous thing. It has a lot of very unusual and peculiar characteristics about it. It cuts the ice, among other things. It has a conning tower far, far above the major hull of the ship, and cutters on the conning tower that cut their way through the ice. I thought at first it was silly, but it works. He couldn't get anybody to back him, and, of course, he needs a couple of hundred million dollars, but he's got quite a bit of backing so far to develop it so I think it will work. He's promised to let me captain the first ship.

Q: It'll take a consortium of oil companies involved in the Arctic, to finance that.

Burke: Well, you can't get a consortium of oil companies on a project that's that nebulous. So this is where he's having trouble. But he might get some mining companies to do it. They can ship out slurry and stuff. He's getting a lot of auxiliary things, a lot of side benefits, from this scheme of his. I helped him work on it initially, just criticized his plans.

Q: Was there any feed-in from the Deep Freeze operation in the Antarctic which was useful in developing this?

Burke: Yes, there were, particularly survival, because all of these people had to know about survival, survival gear, clothing, a lot of things like that. And who was the lad on the West Coast in San Diego, an ice expert?

Q: Waldo Lyon.

Burke: Yes, Waldo Lyon. He, of course, was primarily interested in the Arctic, but he also had been to the Antarctic a great many times, and he--nothing about cold weather operations was ever conducted without letting him have a shot at it.

Q: He was on every one of the expeditions?

Burke: I think he was, he should have been and I think he probably was.

Side 2

Q: Admiral, we began to get involved in the Far East, in Southeast Asia, during the days when you were Chief of Naval Operations. Do you want to focus on that subject, sir?

Admiral Burke: Yes. We got involved in Southeast Asia before then, indirectly, but the most direct reason, most direct cause for the difficulties in Southeast Asia was Korea. As you know, I was on the Military Armistice Committee in Korea, and I was sent out there at the beginning of the Korean War as a troubleshooter, because I had been a troubleshooter in the Navy Department for quite some years and because I'd had a great deal of combat experience and the people who were out there had not had that combat experience. But in the Korean War, it was the first war that we were operating on the defensive, and I don't quite know how that came about, how the attitudes of the Joint Chiefs or the civilian hierarchy or whoever required this, established this procedure, this philosophy, that you could win purely on the defensive. We stayed below the 38th Parallel. This was a big argument as to whether we would cross the 38th Parallel.

Q: Did this happen perchance with the dismissal of MacArthur?

Burke: Before. A long time before. But it was part of the antagonism that was built up back here against MacArthur, and which finally resulted in his dismissal by Truman.

Now, you remember, the 25th--the North Koreans attacked on the 25th of April, I think, across the Imjin River, and the first division they hit was the 25th Division of the Korean Army, that was commanded by General Paik, Sun-yup. At that time he was in his early thirties. The communists just clobbered them. I've gone over his battlefield with him, command posts and where--and he had no artillery, for example,-- where all the little howitzers, mortars, were emplaced--where he had everything. He's got a phenomenal detailed memory of that day.

Q: Etched in his mind.

Burke: Etched in his mind. Thereafter, when we were driven back to the Pusan Perimeter, when the South Koreans were driven back to the Pusan Perimeter and we pulled, by the skin of our teeth, we were able to hold at Pusan, with very, very few damned good soldiers and Marines, mostly Marines because the soldiers unfortunately were garrison troops and had not been trained, and although they were gallant as hell they didn't know how to fight.

Then after the Inchon landing, we had them on the run. And there was a lot of opposition in our government, and I don't know exactly where it came from, to crossing the 38th Parallel. We were going to just defend South Korea. Finally we were permitted to go across the 38th Parallel, but that attitude of not going into the enemy's territory persisted for the rest of the war, and when our troops got up to the Yalu and were driven back, by the Chinese, the people who said we should not have crossed the 38th Parallel had a great field day. They said, "Look, you crossed the 38th Parallel, you had the hell kicked out of you, QED."

It wasn't that simple, but the feeling grew among a

great many people here that we should reach a settlement as soon as possible and not try to operate in the enemy's territories. One of the fundamental elements of war that's been taught by every warrior from time immemorial, from Ghengis Khan all through Clausewitz, Frederick the Great, all of these great captains in the past--in their operations and their thoughts they had a very few simple formulae and they always worked, and one of them is that you hurt the enemy and you don't let him hurt you. Sounds simple. Another is that you operate in the enemy's territory, not your territory, if you can. Another one is, you make the enemy react to your iniative, you do not put yourself where you have to react to the enemy's initiative. Another one is that you cut his supply lines as far back as possible so that he runs out of material. Another one is that you get him in an anvil where you hit him, so that you make him lose his supplies where there is a shortage so that he has to husband his resources or he has to use them and run out of material. These are simple things.

Q: These were enunciated by the great Chinese militarist too, Sun Tsu.

Burke: Yes. Every man in all history who's fought a war comes the same conclusion, if he wins, because that's the way he won. But in Korea. we didn't follow those simple things. We got sophisticated as all hell. Those old principles were no longer applicable or nobody paid any attention to them.

Well, on this Military Armistice Committee that I was on, after we'd kicked hell out of the Chinese and we were driving them back, it became General Hodges' and my job (he's dead now)--it was our job to determine the present line of demarcation, and we refused to accept the present line, present battle line as a final line of demarcation. And the reason why we refused that is, as soon as we took the present battle line as the final line of demarcation it stopped our--there would have been no percentage for us to regain their territory, gain territory and then have to give it up because it was beyond our present battle lines.

So we could bring them, we felt, to the conference table and to an agreement a lot faster if every day we took a little bit of their territory and every day the situation got a little bit worse for them, and it worked. It worked beautifully. It's a long, long story and I don't want to get into it, but we settled in Korea for much less-lesser victory than we could have had, a partial win, and the Chinese, who were in a very bad position, every way, morally, psychologically, militarily, every way possible, they were in a very bad position but they were able to extricate themselves, not through what they did, except at the conference table, but by what we did.

And so we don't want to do what we did in Korea again. We want to handle it a little differently. But we've got the weakness of the Americans. If we can conduct protracted war, if we can keep them on the defensive in their areas, we can win, no question about it. Now, China also needed food. They needed what Southeast Asia had. But they didn't think that if we did enter into any kind of a war in Southeast Asia, that we would do differently than we have done in Korea, and if that was true then they could come out winners.

Q: Was it a factor perhaps that President-elect Eisenhower had gone to Korea and effected the cessation of active warfare, and he was still in office?

Burke: Yes. Yes, this was after we had been ordered to accept the final line of demarcation, the present battle line as the final line of demarcation, and this was when General Hodges and I both refused to carry out our orders three times, and then Ridgeway came over and said, "You are in the military. You are military men. You will carry out your orders."

We said, "That we will do, but we want to be relieved right now, as soon as we do that, because we have lied. We said that our government would never accept these terms, and now we have to go up there and accept them."

"Yes, you do," so we did, and this is a horrible experience.

But anyway, this was a long time before President Eisenhower came in and it was not due to Truman, either. YOu know, Truman's probably done me more harm than any other man alive, and I have great admiration for him, but--

Q: --he tried to do you some harm.

Burke: Yes, but he rectified it, too. He could have done it. He was man enough, without me or anybody, I don't know who did this, but he was man enough to recognize he might have made a mistake, and he changed it, and this takes a big man, because he didn't have to do that. Because I was a little bit of a fellow and I would never have made any squawk about it, but he did it, he corrected an injustice which gained him nothing, the correction--that's a pretty good man. That's why I have admiration for him, and also for MacArthur.

But anyway, this things in Korea, where we had a partial victory and we didn't fight by the old rules of warfare, old maxims of warfare--the Chinese felt that we would do exactly the same thing in Vietnam. Then it turned out, that's exactly what we did. They were right.

Now, there were a lot of weak governments all over Southeast Asia, Burma, India, Thailand, Indochina was broken up into Laos, Vietnam, Cambodia, all of them were weak, and when--I became CNO, by that time there was turmoil in Laos. Vietnam at that time was not in the picture. There was no difficulty, no serious difficulty in Vietnam. More difficulty in Thailand than in Vietnam. Much difficulty in Burma--that was after the Indian affair, where China went into the Assam Plains of India.

You may remember, Laos is a very mountainous country except in the Plaine des Jars, near the Mekong, toward the mouth of the Meking River. There were two villages up in the north of Laos, Sam Neua and Phongsali, if I remember. Anyway those two villages had been communized over a period of years by the Chinese Communists who came in a few at a time and convinced the villages, took over the villages, till they were Communist dominated, and then they made a noise, "We are Communist." Until that time they were very quiet.

Laos had a weak government, weak people, people that we didn't understand, people that negotiated very peculiarly, their morals were not our morals, their combat, the way they fought was not the way we would fight, and Laos was very divided, and the Communists started to come in, the Chinese and North Vietnamese into northern Laos. The Laotian troops, they had only a few, weren't very well trained and they weren't very good and they weren't very well led.

There was a young Laotian captain that defected with his company, Kong Le. He defected to the Communists, and he had been one of the best combat people in the Laotian Army, and this caused tremendous concern, because it created distrust of the whole Laotian Army.

The General in command in Laos was a man named Souvanna Phoumi. He wanted a lot of things. Well, everybody who is on aid wants a lot of things, a lot more than they've got. A lot of people didn't have much confidence in him, and probably well placed. But when you're going to do something in a country, one of the things that you have to find out very early in the game is, who do you support? You have to support an individual and his group. You have to support either a group or an individual. You can't just support a nebulous thing. So it's better not to support anybody, not to do anything, if you're not going to support a group.

Now, when you're going to support a group and you don't fully have confidence in what that group is going to do, then you have to put somebody with that group, an American with that group to--and have the agreements made so that they agree to do what you want done, or you make a mutual agreement of what should be done. Then somebody is there to advise and to report on whether it's being done or not, and to help get in done. That we didn't do. This is what we did with President Magsaysay in the Philippines, and he was a wonderful man and the best president the Philippines has ever had probably, and the man who did that was an Air Force colonel, Colonel Lansdale. He didn't do as well later in Vietnam.

Anyway, we didn't want to really support Souvanna Phoumi, and yet we didn't want the Communists to take over Laos. So we hassled back and forth, again doing a little bit, too little, not properly done, and not wholehearted support of an ally, reluctant support, and it didn't work, and they kept getting cut up by the Communists. Then they had the battle on the Plaine des Jars, they gradually lost it, until it was evident that if we didn't really do something, then we were going to lose Southeast Asia to the Communists. The Communists were going to take it over.

Q: What was our excuse for being there, the SEATO Alliance?

Burke: Yes, the SEATO Alliance and the fact that this was an outside aggression of Communists coming in to take over a people who didn't know how to fight for themselves. It was straight aggression. These people are gentle people.

They didn't know how to fight, didn't want to fight, and it might have been better to let them take them, except the Communists have got a habit, a system of making those people responsive to their desires very fast. They kill quite a few people and the rest of them get the word. So it was a question of Southeast Asia going Communist.

One of the worse things that you can ever do is to commit forces in a country, unless you've got a reasonable chance to win. Well, Laos is not on the seacoast. Laos is an internal country. No navy. And you can't uncommit once you commit there, and so President Eisenhower didn't feel that we should commit forces there, so we didn't. We didn't.

Q: This was a part of his main thesis, that we should never get involved on the mainland.

Burke: Yes. Now, at the end of the Laotian episode, then they started--the Vietcong were increasing the hell they were raising in South Vietnam. The Vietcong, most of them were from the South but there were a great many northerners who came down to help them. It was not just a civil war, It was an aggression, using internal people to upset the country. And so President Eisenhower put advisors in there to help the South Vietnamese Army, particularly Diem. Diem was a hell of a good man, I thought. I had met him. As a matter of fact, I went out to see him a couple of times, nothing important. It was just to keep contact. I think General Eisenhower realized that if you're going to get into a war, of the United States is going to commit its own troops to fight, then you have to commit enough of them to win it, and commit them in such a way as to win it, and this in spite of the fact that he had a great deal to do finally with the forcing of a peace which I think was unsatisfactory in Korea, but still a good deal of that had been done before he took office, too.

But in any case, he had no intention and nobody else had any intention of committing troops to either South Vietnam or Laos. Now, right after President Kennedy took over, I don't know when perhaps in April or May, I was acting chairman and Laos was blowing up very badly. The government group was having the hell beaten out of them, and I went up to brief President Kennedy on the Laotian situation, what I thought about it, and my thesis was, "You can't fiddle with this thing, you can't play with this. This is not a game. If you're going to get into the thing, let's get in and put two or three divisions into Laos, fast, hard-hitting, combat-ready divisions but no occupation troops, you drive the damn Communists out in a hurry by very fast tough operations, real tough, you drive them out. Then you let the

Laotians take it over, and if the Communists come in again, you do it again."

Now, this is a very expensive and very difficult operation to do, because it's not on the seacoast. You have to get troops overland or have to fly them in or something like that. It's very difficult and completely unfamiliar for the United States to have a flying operation, such as the Germans had, the storm trooper idea, and then pull them out, until you get somebody to sign on the dotted line that's had the hell kicked out of them.

But I thought that I had President Kennedy convinced. He made a very strong speech on Laos over the television and used my charts and a good deal of my data, and three days later, he walked back the cat.

I went over to see him about it and said, "Why, Mr. President?" And he said he thought he was wrong in the first place. Well, what had happened was, he'd seen a lot of other people who advised him to continue to do what he was doing. He finally--I argued about it so much that he finally said, "All right, Admiral, I will let you talk to the Congressional leaders, let you discuss this with them and see what they think."

So I did. They all came over to the White House and I made a very impassioned speech, "If you don't fight here, where do you fight? And if you don't fight any place, what's going to happen to Southeast Asia? So we have a choice, the United States has a choice now of getting out of Southeast Asia now, before we are committed to anything, or fighting our way through, which we can win if we do it properly, but you can't go ahead and be part way in and part way out, because you're bound to lose and expend a hell of a lot of people in doing it."

Well, the President went around to everybody. He started with the Vice President, Mr. Johnson. Mr. Johnson said, "I agree with him." He was the last man who said that.

Q: The first and the last.

Burke: Yes. He went all around the table, and some of the people whom I knew must have agreed with me--I think of one, a Senator from New Hampshire, Styles Bridges. . . . I knew damn well that he and others felt that I was right.

So after they'd taken a vote, I asked for a rebuttal, and I gave another impassioned speech and I did this a total of three times, and, of course, I lost completely. So then I went back to my office very disappointed. I immediately went up to the Hill, and I saw this friend of mine, the Senator, and I said, "Senator, I know how you feel. In

God's name, why the hell did you let me stand up there and not support me? When I'm sure that what I said, you would agree with?"

He said, "Sure I do, but you know, it's not the Senate's business to devise strategy. You were sucked into an old, old political game. You should never have agreed to do that, because any Senator that pipes up and says, 'This is correct,' supports the strategy, and thereafter if all of them did it, then it would be the Senate's strategy that the President was putting into effect, and we can't do anything about it, the administration must operate it. All we can do is pass on the strategy that's already been adopted by the administration."

So I learned a lesson.

Q: It isn't exactly the kind of thesis the Senate Foreign Relations Committee adopts, is it?

Burke: Well, it is, yes, because so long as the administration doesn't accept their proposition then they're in a safe position to propose it. The danger comes when the White House says, "All right, we'll do it." And their propositions have been so outlandish that no President can afford to commit the United States to such silly things.

Q: A bit of hypocrisy.

Burke: Sure. Sure there is. This is what I didn't realize, too.

Well, anyway, Mr. Kennedy never again took a realistic view of Southeast Asia. He went in piecemeal, he dabbled, all the time. Now, for example, he never realized when he committed US troops, he never realized he was committing US troops, I'm sure. This was after I left office. But I think the first troops he committed were helicopter troops. But he committed them to combat, and that was bad. You see, if you're going to stick to advising you have to stick just to advising. The military had gotten into the habit, I guess it was a habit by that time, by thinking that if they were to do certain things the logical next step would be taken, too. Inevitably. And it wasn't.

Now, the Vietnam War, the unfortunate part about the Vietnam War is that the United States as a nation never supported anybody. We could have supported Diem. We didn't. We undercut Diem. Diem was not perfect, he had a lot of things wrong with him, but we could have put somebody alongside of him to have separated him from his brother's wife, Madame Nu--a brilliant and a very clever woman and beautiful too--we could have put a Colonel Lansdale in there. We should actually have put Colonel Lansdale in with Diem at that time or somebody like him, and we could have persuaded Diem to be reasonable about the things he was doing and the things he was not doing. We got all mixed up with religion, and we swallowed the Communist propaganda, and we let Diem die if we didn't actually help kill him. We never supported him. We never supported anybody else. Even now we aren't really supporting Thieu. And yet, the success of South Vietnam is dependent upon the success of the leaders of South Vietnam, and if we let one leader after another go, about the third time, the third leader is going to say, "To hell with this," and he's going to double cross us.

That's one thing. The other thing is, if we had wanted--when we've committed ourselves to military action, in South Vietnam, we should have committed ourselves to destroying North Vietnam--which we could have done. We could have fought in the enemy's territory, instead of landing at Danang, as a main landing, and that being the farthest north place we had, we should have landed up in North Vietnam. We should have put a small detachment, a battalion or maybe a division, of striking force landed south of Hanoi and raised hell for a couple of months, destroying the military installations around there and destroying their ability to conduct war. We should have made them react to our surprise moves, and then we should have pulled out, quickly, and said to the South Vietnamese, you handle it now, and if they couldn't if the Communists came in again, we go back in again. This may happen two or three times, and then we should have trained the South Vietnamese to fight right away. The Vietnamization started much too late, as it did in Korea. But basically, we wanted to play at war, and war is nothing to play with. It's a very dangerous desparate game, that has been studied over and over again by experts, but unfortunately your group, historians, don't really believe the old lesson. It's been proved every time, just as we proved once again, the validity of things that were proved a thousand years ago, about the conduct of war. Too bad, because Mr. Kennedy, who I think was a very bad President because I think he was misled by a great many people, but he himself was not a bad man. I liked Jack Kennedy. I thought he was a very fine man. But he permitted himself to jeopardize the nation, without being willing to carry through on an operation, and he did this over and over. He did it at the Bay of Pigs. He did not do it on the missile crisis. He did a good job there. However, he knew damn well what the score was before he started. This was all right. But he did it in Vietnam, and Johnson followed through and did exactly the same thing, except that Johnson had the right idea at one time.

Q: He expressed it in this meeting, when you addressed

them.

Burke: Yes, but after that, when he was President he tried to do the right thing, but he didn't have the power. His power in the Presidency was not enough for him to carry through on the thing, because he wanted to be popular and correct, and sometimes I think it's impossible to be both.

But this Vietnam War is a very sad thing. It's not the cause of all the difficulties that we're experiencing. It's not the cause, as many people say it is, but it is another effect of a basic inability to look at real things, to take a realistic view of what is, not what you'd like to have it be.

Q: How valid was this oft expressed fear that if we did anything more in Vietnam in those early days, the Red Chinese might get involved? How valid was that, how convinced were people that this was possible?

Burke: Well, many people were convinced of that. And the reason again is because Americans who haven't been in Oriental or foreign countries a lot have an idea that everybody thinks alike, that we're all equal in the way we think, and it's not true. Communists are realistic people. They're a bunch of bastards but they're realistic. And they aren't going to go to war because you come close, or they aren't going to go to war because you're operating in a third country's territory, unless they have good reason to go to war anyway. Not for that reason. They wouldn't have gone to war just because we'd operated in North Vietnam. They would have gone to war if they'd thought they could have kicked the hell out of us in a hurry and have us capitulate. They would have gone to war then. But they would not have gone to war just because we entered. So what we did was to measure the intent, the possible intent of the enemy, by our own beliefs. The US might have done something like that. Because we've been misread that way before. We went into two world wars when our enemies didn't expect us to, and our tendency is to do, to defend something like that, but not them. They very reason why our enemies felt before in two world wars we would not go to war was the very reason why I think that the Chinese Communists would not have come in. In the second place, they didn't have the military power to be successful. Now, before that time, Mao Tse-tung had laid down his principle, 'war is protracted conflict,' and the sayings of Mao in the "Little Red Book" (I've got his "Little Red Book" here some place, pretty good book, not bad). He had measured us pretty well in that book. I don't think there really was any danger.

War is not something that most nations play with.

We do. But most nations don't.

Q: At one stage we permitted the kind of secret arm of our government, the CIA, to get involved in a military operation in Laos. Was this not thought to be something that might incite the Chinese?

Burke: Well, it could incite them but it wouldn't cause them to go to war. Now, this is where we made a mistake. We made a mistake because the CIA has been eminently successful in other operations in other parts of the world. They had too much faith in some of their own operators, who were not capable of carrying out the operation, maybe nobody was capable of it, I don't know, but--now, that's an irritating damn thing, all right, to have another nation's secret service secretly conducting guerilla war or any type or war against you. But it's done all the time. In Ireland, in northern Ireland now, I'm sure that somebody is supporting the IRA. It may not be the Soviets, it may be somebody else, but the IRA is being supported, because it's not being supported by the Dublin government and yet they have a lot of equipment and they're doing very well. Those people are paid in the IRA. They're paid well.

In Cypress both the Turks and the Greeks are conducting clandestine operations against the ohter. In this country right now the Soviets and the Red Chinese are doing everything they can to control the most important aspects of our operations against them--which is the way we think. What we will do. In other words, to try to change our intent. They're expert at this. They're very good. Now, it isn't all due to them by any means, but they take advantage of this and this goes down into elementary countries like the fight down in East Africa. Zambia and the nation right to the north, Tanzania. Zambia sent an expeditionary force across, called them insurrectionaries, and they got the hell kicked out of them but Tanzania killed the whole damn works--and a lot of other people, too. While the ruler of Tanzania was about it he thought he might as well get rid of all of his enemies and he did. They fight wars in a very elementary way by killing the whole damn bunch, everybody that might oppose them and, of course, this creates the condition for future war. Somebody overthrows them and kills them.

Q: It must be somewhat irritating to legitimate military figures in a country to have these operations going on sub rosa.

Burke: It is. It is, because you never--no man who's in active military service likes the subversive, that kind of warfare, that kind of operation. It goes against the grain. But yet some of those operations were quite successful. The thing that used to gripe me, it happened several times, was when a CIA operation was about to fail, the first time I would hear about it would be when it was about to fail and they would say, "Can you do this?" Rescue them. Then you'd go in and rescue them. And that gripes the hell out of me, too, but you've got to do it, because it's the United States, and some of those operations were never heard of.

Q: These days, in that part of the world, guerilla warfare is a fairly new and accepted technique, isn't it, has to be?

Burke: Yes, guerilla warfare is fairly new, it's about 5000 years old. Exactly the same thing. What we have forgotten is that warfare extends through a gambit of operations, and guerilla warfare behind the enemy's lines is a pretty good thing. We used it even in the Civil War and we've used it in most wars, but we've got in the habit of using tanks and frontal attack and big armies. Both World War I and II, we forgot the use of guerilla warfare, because we didn't contribute much to guerilla warfare. The other nations, European nations, did but we did not.

Q: It's reborn--for us.

Burke: Reborn. You always have to find--every new group that comes into office has got to re-invent the wheel and find all the wonderful things they can do. Like mass production of things, like the Navy goes into this great program building all the ships alike, as something brand new, yet the first ships we ever did were the frigates about 1795 and they tried to build them all alike and that failed, too.

Q: In Southeast Asia, we had gone in, in an economic way, working in the hamlets. Was this begun during the Eisenhower administration, did we think of helping them economically?

Burke: Yes, but we didn't have the technique of being able to do it well. We don't have it yet. For example, if you want to help, this goes to private charities or anything else, I think the only way you can help any group of people who are disadvantaged or whatever you want to call them is to get them first with the willingness ot help themselves, and secondly to give them the skills with which to do it. But they come in that order, they've got to be willing to help themselves. There's no amount of money you can pour into anything and cure anything if you don't have somebody who wants to spend it wisely, as we have found out in urban renewal and other of our own social projects in this country. But the same thing is even more true when you're dealing with foreigners. It's very hard to convey an idea that you want to help them, and yet you're not going to give them unlimited support. Did I tell you about the Ecuadorian Naval Academy?

Q: No.

Burke: Well, when I was CNO, Ecuador who had a very small but a very good little Navy, they had sent their people, naval officers up here for years for post graduate education, and they always stood well in their class. And so I heard the plans by the Chief of Staff of the Ecuadorean Navy, Chief of Naval Staff, who got the information to me that Ecuador needed a new naval academy--they needed a naval academy.

So I scouted around, sent somebody down, or something, anyway I found out that their naval academy was a group of little chicken coops. Really their buildings were not much better than chicken coops, little frame buildings. They were god-awful.

Q: Where was it?

Burke: Down near Guayaquil off the mouth of the Guayaquil River. It was bad. It was bad. So I got some photographs taken, got data, and I was about to be visited by the Chief of Naval Staff of Ecuador, and I knew that what he was going to ask me for was a naval academy. And it would come to quite a few millions of dollars, I don't know how much but he had quite elaborate ideas of what they would like to have for a naval academy.

He came up here. I didn't know what the hell to do in the beginning, but then I went back to this fundamental thing, that you can't do any good for anybody unless they want to do it, and so when he asked me about that, he wanted us to build it, I said, "No, Admiral. Tell you what I'm going to do. I will send you four officers to help you build your naval academy and I will give you, not loan you, give you second hand equipment that you don't have in Ecuador like generators or wiring or something like that. It won't be new equipment, it will be equipment that we'll take off of our ships and might possibly have scrapped, but they will be usable, and you use your troops, your people, to build the naval academy. These four people we'll send down, I don't know who they are but they'll be young people who are knowledgeable technical people and they'll work under your supervision. They will work for you, but they will know how. If you want a naval academy you can build it."

And it hurt him like hell, but finally they did, and

they built that naval academy. It was commissioned just before I retired. They built this thing all by themselves and they never had more than four officers down there, and these were kids who knew how to make concrete, how to make concrete blocks, how to build buildings, and--young engineers, and they were good. They got along well and they learned Spanish, and they had tremendous responsibilities. It was a great challenge to them. They could direct great construction crews. In a year and a half they built their naval academy, which looks much like a big motel. Very good. I went down to commission it. The Ecuadorean government invited me down and they named it Burke Ecuadorean Naval Academy. Of course, that name went off the next day. But-- it had a brass plate on it, they took the brass plate off but I've got a copy of the brass plate some place.

They were very proud of that, and they should be, because they'd worked like hell to build that naval academy. It's their naval academy. They've got it now, and they've got a better naval academy, it's in good shape, they've got a better naval academy than they would ever have had no matter how much money we'd poured into it, because they did it.

Q: It must have given you great satisfaction to know that your thesis worked.

Burke: Oh yes. I got in some difficulties because there was an Indian boy born the day that I was down there, little Catholic boy, and the father wrote and asked me if I would become his godfather. I said I would, but I didn't know that a Protestant could be the godfather of a Catholic, because I didn't know what Catholic godfathers were required to do. It's different. He got special dispensation or whatever he got, I don't know how far up he had to go to get it, but anyway I got authority from the Catholic Church.

Q: He probably got it from the archbishop.

Burke: Maybe. Anyway I got to be godfather of this boy, and later on I had lots of difficulties. Their idea of being godfather is to take over the child, and that's not quite what I wanted to do.

Q: Certainly in time of need, their idea is to take him over completely--

Burke: That would be all right, I've done that for a couple of kids, but I don't want to take him over when the need isn't there. They had more money than I had. That wasn't the idea.

Q: In connection with that, if you had gone forward with the Admiral's initial request and it would cost several million dollars, would this have come out of the Navy budget?

Burke: No, that would have come out of aid. I would have fought for that in our aid budget, which wouldn't have been a naval budget. It wasn't a question of our money, it was a question of building a real naval academy with a real pride.

Q: I understand that, I was asking what the principle or policy was because there must have been many other requests of various natures which would come to you.

Burke: Well, there were a lot of them. The Ethiopians, for example, wanted a ship, wanted a yacht for the Emperor. He finally got it, over my opposition but he got it. Latin American countries all wanted cruisers. I saw no reason why we didn't give them cruisers. We were going to scrap them anyway. Let them have it. Turkey wanted cruisers and Greece, for each other--why not give them two cruisers each? That would be balanced. That would make them both happy. We weren't going to use them, we'd junk them.

Things like that don't cost anything. The thing that bothered me was, when you gave them money and they didn't have to do anything for it--this was bad!

Q: Bad for an individual as well as a nation. Some of

them wanted to reach a little higher than cruisers, didn't they?

Burke: Oh yes. They wanted aircraft carriers. Brazil wanted an aircraft carrier. It finally got the MINAS GERAS from Britain, and that caused us a great deal of trouble, because of the aviation fight down there between naval aviators and the air force. As a matter of fact, one time President Kubitschek--the Minister of the Navy was a man named Mattoso Maia, naval officer, admiral, very fine man, still alive. He called me up on the telephone, which was unusual in those days and said, "Please come to Brazil."

I said, "I can't!" "You've got to." Finally I went down there, 12 hours to fly down, I was there in Brasilia for 12 hours, flew back for 12 hours in an old DC-6.

Q: What a strenuous trip.

Burke: Yes. For about a two-hour conference with the president of Brazil on behalf of amicable relations.

Q: They never did resolve that struggle between navy and air force, did they?

Burke: Yes, they resolved it, and about the way I proposed it.

Q: Did they have to have planes for the carrier?

Burke: Yes. I suggested that the Navy operate the carrier, but that anybody, any individual regardless of service who could qualify on carriers (and the service permitted you to qualify on carriers and operate from carriers) should be permitted to do so. If they'd done that in the beginning it would have been all right. And they did it finally. I don't know what's happened now.

Q: Was it during your regime, the policy of every two years senidng a task force to Latin America for training purposes?

Burke: Yes, the Amity Cruise.

Q: Amity Cruise--and that was something during your time?

Burke: Yes, except I did it every year (starting about 1957) I think for a while, which was too much, to get it started. And that was so that we could operate. We sent our old ships down there, kind of ships they had in Latin America but their ships were no good. So first cruise, we sent our ships down there, with technical people, to know, to learn people more than anything else, learn how they operated, and in the long range was to get their navy operating together, to increase the effectiveness of their navy, to get them so they knew one another and knew us.

Q: Kind of a naval mission afloat.

Burke: Yes, and it turned out to be very, very good, so good that they do operate pretty well together and naval officers know each other. I started the same thing around Africa, but it doesn't work around there simply because they have no navies and it's a different group of people, not just a different attitude but--Latin Aermicans are very fine people and they will help, but Africans want to get what they can and to hell with you.

Q: Actually they haven't reached that stage of development, have they?

Burke: There's that. But there are a lot of things that I tried to start, and some of them have been very successful. A lot of these things improved the operations, the support of one country to another, and by improving mutual support among navies, and to do that you must know people. You must know how they operate and how they think, so every time I could I'd have mutual operations with other navies whether we were allied with them or not. Starting with the Mexicans, we exchanged instructors in the Naval Academy--young Mexican lieutenant I brought up as my aide and sent him to the Naval Academy, not to teach Spanish but to teach American naval history, because our young American boys who see a Mexican teaching our naval history are a hell of a lot more impressed than if he teaches what he should know, like Spanish. Now we've got him back to teaching language again. But even that does some good.

The Naval Command Course in the Naval War College, the communications systems that I set up with Collins Radios in Latin America so that every CNO had automatic communication with every other one every morning, and usually talked about the weather, but it still helped, because that too, is unofficial communications business,--sometimes there would be jokes passed over. The relationships between the people then who were CNOs then--the personal relationships--here's (Professor R.) Ruge, for example, who sends me everything he writes. It happens to be a series of--

Here, this is from another one, this is from the Swedish CNO, came in yesterday--

Q: You were like a naval United Nations Secretariat.

Burke: I still am--not that way. They're friends. They're damn good friends. If you read that letter, you'll find things he wouldn't say to anybody but a Swede in there, at times. I won't use it, I'm not going to--

Q: A very satisfying kind of accomplishment, I would think.

Burke: This is the basis of internal and external operations. You've got to get people to operate together, and you've got to support people who are trying, and you've got to kick hell out of the people who don't try. But first you've got to know where the hell you're going.

I think you've now reached the part where he's critical of the Swedish government, Swedish Navy. Yet he is Commander-in-Chief of it.

Q: That's a remarkable letter, from such a person.

Burke: There are probably some more in that pile that I haven't read but these are--this is what so many people forget, that you end up with people, and if you've got good people and they trust you and you can trust them and they're all working for a purpose that's beyond anything in their own individual advancement, you can get a hell of a lot done. And you can't get it done any other way.

Burke 4 - 192

Interview with Admiral Arleigh Burke
by John T. Mason, Jr.

January 12, 1973
Washington, D. C.

Q: Admiral, last time when you concluded your remarks, you were talking about your international relations, the fact that you had established working relations and personal relations with a great number of naval figures in other countries. I wonder if you want to continue on that subject a little bit?

Admiral Burke: Yes, I would, because this has been one of the most satisfying things in my whole life. The last time we talked was before Christmas. Now it's several weeks after, and I have a lot of Christmas cards from my old friends who are still alive, from Admiral Ruge of Germany, from the Japanese, from Husvedt of Norway, Erisson of Sweden, Clement of the Argentine, Mattoso-Maia of Brazil. And I've forgotten the name of the man from South Africa who's now on active duty and is chariman of the Joint Chiefs down there now. He's been there 20 years, I guess. A very wonderful man.

This thing started quite by accident, I think. When I took over as CNO, Admiral Carney had already asked Admiral Louis Mountbatten, who was First Sea Lord of the Royal Navy, to be his house guest when he came to the United

States. And he asked me if I would take over his invitation. I said, of course, I would, and so Admiral and Lady Mountbatten came over, stayed with us, and we exchanged a terrific amount of information. No one item was very important, but we got a lot of little information, of how things were going, what they were trying to do, what was happening in the world, what they thought of various things, and it was quite valuable.

I had known Louis Mountbatten before, but this was very helpful. So, partially as a result of that and partially because everybody knows it's good to know the people you're dealing with, I had a schedule made up of all the CNOs of all the "free world" to come to the United States, a rough schedule, and more or less in the order of importance, to the United States.

For example, early in the game came the Japanese and the Germans. Then there were the NATO countries, and then the Latin American countries, and then the Middle East countries, and India.

Q: Interesting that you put at the top of the list the former enemies.

Burke: That is right, because they were having trouble. They were having trouble re-forming and they were unsure, they were defeated and they knew they were defeated. If we didn't give them good advice and real help, they might stray. They might get antagonistic or they might get resentful. A lot of things might happen. And they needed help to re-form not only their Navy but their governments.

These were all working trips. Up until that time, they'd been largely ceremonial. They would come over, and they would have big parties. They would go to New York and see a couple of good shows. They would also visit naval installations. But I stopped everything but the working part, so that they would deal with the things that they wanted to see. They would see professional people in their own profession, and very little outside of the Navy unless they particularly wanted to.

Q: They came as guests of our government?

Burke: Yes. They paid their way over normally, but while they were here, they were guests of our Navy, all their expenses were paid here. Usually individuals put them up, like I put them up frequently in the quarters, and sometimes I didn't, sometimes they stayed in hotels but in that case we footed the bill. Once in a while, if we had planes, for example from Pakistan, Pakistan couldn't at that time afford to send their CNO over here, so if we had a plane

coming back, why,--had a regularly scheduled plane, a MATS--
we would ask them if they would mind coming over on that
sort of a plane. And they all appreciated this working
business, and it worked.

The first visit, of course, was sort of preliminary.
You get a lot out of it, but you don't really get down to
understanding what's behind what they're trying to do, on
the first visit. So it takes several. Sometimes they
came here first. Sometimes I went to their country first.
But most of them I saw a great many times, one way or another,
over the six years.

Now, you take Mattoso-Maia for example, who's been
retired about as long as I have, and we still correspond
occasionally. Mattoso-Maia called me up one day and said,
"Could you please come to Brazil?" On, I think, a Thursday
or Friday or something. I said, "I can't, Admiral."

He said, "It's very important that you come down here
very soon."

I said, "Admiral, my schedule is just blocked, I can't
do it. I just can't do it."

He said, "You only have to be here for a little while."

I said, "Admiral, the only time that I have off is
this weekend."

He said, "Can you come down this weekend?"

I said, "Yes, I could."

He said, "I'd appreciate it very much."

So I went down there. It's a 12 hour flight. This is when we had the old prop planes, of course. That's all we had and it was a 12 hour flight.

Q: It sounds exceedingly difficult.

Burke: So I bundled my wife up and we took off for Brazil, and we went down to Brasilia, and I didn't know what it was all about. Brasilia then was unformed. They were trying to get governmental officers, Brazilian governmental officers to Brasilia, but they didn't want to go. The Navy Department was about half there and the President was in Brasilia, so--it was a dreary place, but beautiful even then. The streets weren't finished and the buildings weren't finished, but you could see it was going to be a beautiful spot.

Anyway, I got down. We were met in Brasilia--no, I think we had to land in Rio because the airfield in Brasilia wasn't big enough and then the Brazilian Air Froce took us to Brasilia. I think that was it. Anyway, Mattoso-Maia met us and I said, "What in the hell is this all about?"

He said, "I want you to talk with the President about our aircraft carrier. We're having a lot of trouble," and they were, because of a big squabble in their services between the naval aviators and the Air Force, and they had a carrier which they had purchased from Britain, and we had trained some of their naval aviators, and Kubitschek was President of Brazil, was about to make a decision as to who would fly the aircraft off of the carrier.

So we got to our hotel room and he stopped talking. I said, "Do you want to contine this?"

He said, "Let's take a walk." And so we went out into a field, walked around the field, and I said, "What the hell is the matter?"

He said, "I can never tell whether anything's bugged around here or not. But I know that this field's not bugged."

So he said, "I'd like to have you tell Kubitschek by yourself what you think."

I said, "Well, Admiral, I'm not going to get into an internal fight in Brazil. I'm going to lay out what might happen and the possible compromises. What I will probably end up with is recommending that anyone who is qualified to fly from the carrier, be permitted to fly."

He said, "I wouldn't like that."

I said, "Well, that's probably what I would do because I don't want to get mixed up in a fight between your air force and your navy. It's not my--I shouldn't do that."

He said, "I understand that."

Well, we only had about an hour, I guess, because when I went in to see President Kubitschek and explained the advantages and disadvantages as I saw them to various aspects of the argument, he asked a lot of questions. I finished, had lunch with Mattoso-Maia, was out there about 12, 14 hours, I think in Brasilia, and then we came back to Washington.

Q: Did you make any contact with our naval mission there?

Burke: Yes. Yes, but that was all. I didn't have time for anything but just to make contact, make my number and get out. But I don't think I did Mattoso-Maia very much good or the Brazilian Navy, or very much good at all. But the nice part about that was that he could feel that we were friends, personal friends enough that he could call on me for help.

Q: It's a tremendous favor he asked.

Burke: It was. It was, and this was why he's never forgotten it. He never will. In Brazil, he would support us when it was possible to do so. He would help us on Amity Cruises. He would do everything he could to make things go nicely between our two countries.

Now, the same thing happened in Germany. Ruge, who by the way was Rommel's naval Chief of Staff before the landing, and Ruge was primarily a mine-sweeping officer. They had a mine-sweeping force in Germany after the war which they retained to get the mines clear of their harbors. But they had no navy, and they were to start a navy. They couldn't start a navy from scratch. They couldn't do very much without our approval, the Allies' approval.

So I asked Ruge, who I knew was appointed inspector general of the Navy, to come over. I always asked them what they wanted to see, what they were interested in so we could set things up of value to them. He was primarily interested in small ships, of course. We had a great deal to do with the forming of the German Navy. We didn't have very much to do with forming the German Defense Department, and the Defense Department was under the domination of the German Army, as all these things in Germany always have been.

But we had a lot to do with the formation of the navy he followed the suggestions we made for the kinds of ships, what could Germany do in war, not right away but gradually, how could they improve their capabilities, their support of what all our Allies could do?

So the net result of that in the long run, I gave them three ships from my own DesRon 23. I said, "You take care of these ships." "They fought a lot of good battles for us, maybe they'll fight some good ones for you, but you take care of them."

Well, they appreciated that. And we helped them a lot.

Q: These were outright gifts.

Burke: Yes. And they paid us for things, too. They bought weapons systems. We trained their crews. I remember going down to Charleston to see the commissioning of one of the ships that we did give them, the takeover from American crews to German crews, and when the German crews formed on the dock and marched down to the ship, I had the band play "Lili Marlene," which was forbidden in the German Navy, forbidden in Germany, and you could see the tears come in their eyes.

Well, things like that were very good. Ruge is now a professor in the University of Tubingen in Germany. His wife has died. I know all of his children. He comes over here. He probably will be over here in a year or so. He's an old friend. He will stay with us. He'll get up and make his own breakfast, take his own walks, and if he has an idea he will carry it out. We're good friends.

When it came time to select his successor, he asked me to come over there and help him do it. I said, "No, I won't do that." But he said, "I'd like you to come over and look and meet everyone, every captain and admiral in the German Navy."

Q: That's a large order, too.

Burke: Well, there weren't very many at that time. Which I did, and he selected the right man. He had some good people.

But this was worthwhile. Same thing is true with the Japanese Navy. I'm very greatly honored when I learned by a letter I just got from Commander J. E. Auer of our own Navy who's a Japanese language student over there. He's now ComNav FE. I learned from his letter about the exhibit at Ita Jima, which is a school, naval academy--and they have a lot of my speeches translated in that exhibit and on the bulkhead, as the Father of the Japanese Navy. (Matter of fact, I hope the speeches are really good).

But this was because of the close personal relationship between (me and) Admiral Hoshina and Admiral Nomura. Admiral Hoshina still writes to me on the situation in Japan and has been a member of the Diet. Now he's 83. The Japanese have a very high regard for him. And the formation of the Japanese Navy that started when I was over there at the beginning of the Korean War. They had a mine-sweeping force. As a matter of fact, I think I ought to have you read Auer's article that's going to be sent to the NAVAL INSTITUTE. I'll run a copy for that. It contains a little bit of information about this.

But I met with Hoshina and Nomura quite often at the beginning, and outlined a rough idea of what their Defense Department should look like, what their Navy should be, and I recommended to them, "Don't let anybody try to form in a vacuum, in an ivory tower, the details of what kind of a navy you're going to try to develop even initially. What you must do, I think, is to get ten officers, ten of the very best people you know in Japan, get them, appoint them. That's your most important duty. Then after you get those ten officers, give them the job of determining what kind of a Navy is possible and what kind of a Navy then can devise. If there's a core of any military force it's the officers' corps. If you get good officers, you've got a good navy. You don't have to worry about the materielle in the ships or the aircraft or tactics or anything like that, get the people who will be good and require other people who come in to be good, too."

This is how Admiral Nagasawa was appointed Chief of DEF-For. Seagoing Self Defense Force. He was a wonderful man. He's dead now. I still get letters from every chief who's alive, once a year from every ex-CNO, ex-Chief of Staff.

Q: The men you dealt with the the fifties.

Burke: Well, men since then. Uchida, for example, who's just been retired. He was one time Chief of the Naval Staff and then became Chairman of the Joint Chiefs. Those are not the correct titles, but the positions correspond to ours. They still write every year, all of them. It gets tiresome sometimes. This is why I have such a hell of a correspondence. I don't write long letters, but even short ones--they deserve an answer. The Greeks and the Turks, for example, they have always been at each other's throats for a couple of hundred years, and they both want ships. You have to help them equally and you have to help them the way they want to be helped, except that you've always got to make sure that they understand that you're going to do exactly the same thing for the Greeks, for the Turks, for the other one.

When the Greeks took over a couple of our destroyers,

Queen Fredericka came over to accept the ships. Now, I've know Queen Fredericka for a long time and I knew all of their navy people, their senior navy people whose names mostly I can't pronounce now. Queen Fredericka stayed with us in the quarters. But she was furious at her ambassador, because the ambassador had told her that he thought it was not appropriate for a woman to accept men-of-war, and she-- we were in a receiving line in my house. We had a dinner for her and then after a dinner we had a reception for people, we couldn't have that many for dinner, and we were in a receiving line, and I guess, the Ambassador, Alexis S. Liatis apparently had talked to her right after dinner, before the reception started, and by the time she got in the receiving line, she was furious. And a furious woman is bad enough, but a furious Queen is pretty bad.

I was next to her, of course, and she said, "Admiral, I must talk to you soon by yourself."

I said, "Yes, Your Majesty, but this reception is about to begin."

She said, "Can we excuse ourselves for a few minutes?"

I said, "Certainly," so we went over into the little sun room that we have there, and I said, "What can I do for you?"

She said, "Well, how do you like my ambassador."

I said, "I think he's a fine man."

She said, "I think he's terrible and I'm about to fire him right now. I'm about to send him home."

I said, "Why?"

"He told me that I should not give this speech day after tomorrow in San Diego accepting these ships, that I should give a little short general speech and then let him or some man, some other representative of Greece."

I said, "Well, Your Majesty, I think that's---"

She said, "So I think I will discharge him and send him home right now."

I said, "Don't do that, Your Majesty, please don't do that. He's a good man. He's made a mistake on this, he's wrong on this," (and I thought he was). "He's wrong on this, but you give the speech and give him hell, but don't humiliate him. It won't do Greece any good or you any good or anybody any good."

She was still furious, but she didn't send him back. She went out there, and we gave a party for her in San Diego or Long Beach. First on the ship, she accepted the ships and she gave one of the most beautiful speeches (it's some place in my files I'm sure), that I've ever heard from a sovereign to her people, to her navy people. It was very good. Of course, they have a religious ceremony on their ships, too.

Then she said on the way out, we went out in our plane, "Could we please not have too many, too big parties?"

I said, "All right, we'll do that, but we've got to have one big one so mayors, governors and people can come. We'll have a reception."

"But not these long, long dinners."

"No--what kind of a dinner would you like?"

She said, "I would like a dinner that you would give if I weren't here."

I said, "All right, I will have a dinner of naval officers and their wives, and you'll come as a naval officer's wife. Would that be all right?"

She said, "That would be lovely."

So at the dinner I introduced her as a naval officer's wife, and let "Her Majesty" go, and before the night was over, her daughter was there, too, both of her daughters. Before the night was over she was asking people to call her Fredericka. I had to make a point of making a little speech and saying, "Your Majesty, as long as those doors are closed, that's all right. Any time that you go out of that door or those doors are opened, it is Your Majesty."

She said, "You uphold my dignity well."

But this was valuable. All of these things were valuable because of the little things that demanded a friendship between countries.

Q: And because you could make them so. Your personality was involved.

Burke: No, it wasn't so much that. It's the amount of effort. Personality doesn't enter into it very much. It takes a lot of effort to do something like that. It takes a lot of--well, I guess understanding, because things don't happen the way you'd like to have them happen.

Q: It certainly took a lot of physical effort. That Brazilian trip required stamina.

Burke: All of those things--a CNO's got to have stamina. He ought to have brains, but he's got to have stamina.

Q: All of these things add up to the next point I'd like to talk about, and that is your re-appointment in late 1959 for a most unusual third term as Chief of Naval Operations. Tell me about that. Your reluctance to accept--

Burke: Well, I was quite reluctant to accept the re-appointment. I had been asked by the President and the SecDef and the Secretary of the Navy--

Q: --that was Gates by that time, was it not?

Burke: No, I don't think so. I think it was still McElroy. But maybe. And I didn't want to accept very much. You're caught on something like that. It's a great honor and anybody would want that sort of an honor. It's a great privilege. But there were a lot of nice things about being re-appointed, but there's a lot of things that can go very wrong, too. In the first place, it can be bad for a man to stay too long in a top spot. It stifles some sort of promotion. You get stagnant in the job. You get a feeling that you've studied that problem before and you already know the answer, when the answer might be different. You're stereotyped in Congress, your relationship to Congress. And besides that you get very tired. It takes a lot of stamina for that job. You work seven days a week and you're lucky if you can get seven hours sleep a night, and you have lot of social work in addition to other work. Your personal life is nil. So all and all, I thought for the good of the Navy, I ought to retire.

Nobody can judge himself, whether he's any good or not. Because you've seen an awful lot of people who stay on a job, both in civilian life and military, stay on too long, and then nobody wants to tell them frankly, "You're overstaying your usefulness."

I'm having a little difficulty persuading a man in

civilian life now, who's a very important man--he believes that because he's reached 70, he should retire. Actually he's very important to the company, but he doesn't want to stay on too long. Well, I can't persuade him that he's not going to. He knows he's not staying on too long now, but he doesn't know when that time will come. Well, the only thing that will make him stay on, I'm sure, is for me to arrange for a committee to be appointed that will tell him frankly when he ought to get out.

Now, I had these same thoughts, too, that I ought to get out. My personal desire was to get out,--I wanted to be home a little bit, I've got a nice wife, I want to keep her, and I was tired. But the big thing that I was fearful of was, people were just being kind to me and generous and saying polite things and they didn't really mean it. I don't know how you can evaluate things like that.

Q: But you also had a committee wait upon you, did you not?

Burke: Yes, I had a committee. They wrote memoranda and things which are in the files some place. But finally they got together with Chester Ward, the JAG, and he cut a tape of the reasons --

Q: -- these were all naval officers?

Burke: Yes. The reasons why I should stay on. And it was a

very persuasive tape, because I played that several times. I even played it for my wife, and she said that they were just hitting my soft spots, which was true. But actually what convinced me finally was when I went over to see President Eisenhower, and he didn't try to argue at all, he just said, "It's your duty."

Q: Your duty--military.

Burke: Yes. He said, "It's your duty to stay," and that ended it.

But I don't think six years is advisable normally. Surely, there are a lot of good people in the Navy, an awful lot of them, and a lot of them can take over that job and do an adequate job. There are some that can do it better than others, but there were a lot --

When I finally did retire, I had trouble the next time, too, as I knew I was going to, so I submitted my request for retirement before the election, before Mr. Kennedy, so that there wouldn't be any political connations about it. And then after Mr. Connolly was SecNav, and Mr. McNamara SecDef, President Kennedy wanted me to stay on. But that I knew would be wrong. I had no doubt then that I ought to get off. And besides that I had done all the preliminary steps before I knew who was going to be President, so there were no political connotations to that at all.

Q: In those latter years there were a number of very interesting things that happened. I wonder if you'd comment on them. In '60 while the Eisenhower Administration was still in, we had this unexpected fire on the CONSTELLATION in the New York shipyard, and you were there.

Burke: Not at the fire. I went up there as soon as I heard there was a fire, and a lot of people were hurt. This was a fire in the shipyard. The ship had a lot of civilian workmen aboard and a very few crew, if I remember rightly, and nearly all the people who were hurt were civilians. But what I couldn't understand was how the hell a fire like that could get started and why it should go so long, and why the firemen could not get to it, and I couldn't get a very good answer. So I went up.

Well, there was a lot of trouble with jurisdiction. I didn't know there were jurisdictional disputes among fire companies or among different types of fire fighters, and among different areas, but there were. Part of it was that. Part of it was because they didn't have the equipment ready to fight a fire in confined spaces, particularly an electrical fire. But they did a pretty good job after they once got started. The fire got under way too long before the fire companies really went to work.

The interesting thing about that was, I went to a civilian hospital in which these people were, the workmen, and I had been very disappointed in naval hospitals, by cleanliness, care, records, administration in general of hospitals, which is not very good. But I had the chief nurse of this hospital in Brooklyn--the chief nurse took me around, and I've never seen anything quite as bad. A field hospital was better. It was dirty. So I asked her about it. She, of course, felt exactly the way I did. But it was very hard to get doctors. The administration was very poor. The doctors didn't want to be administrators. They couldn't get anyone else who was capable. They didn't have enough nurses. Their records were not kept very well. It took a long time to get the information from X-rays to operating doctors and a whole lot of stuff like that, unless individuals follow through. So I came back feeling that naval hospitals were not so bad after all.

But the people that were burned were not burned badly, most of them were just light burns. They put them in the hospital to make sure that nothing happened. And this was sound.

Q: You also visited some of the families of those who were killed.

Burke: Well, yes. That's always hard to do. It's something that's appreciated, but it's very hard on the families too, to have such people visit them, yet in the long run they appreciate it.

Q: A rather unique role for a Chief of Naval Operations.

Burke: No. No, I think you always ought to go where the trouble is, if you can help.

Q: In January of 1961, no, it was in June, there was the incident involving the Portuguese ship that was taken over by a dissident group, the SANTA MARIA.

Burke: Oh---my old friend, yes.

Q: Tell me about that.

Burke: Who was that, who was the---Portuguese admiral?

Q: Admiral H. Malta Galvao and General H. Delgado.

Burke: Galvao had been---I either met him here when he was some sort of attache here, or I met him in Portugal. I knew him. He was a very ardent man, of course, and he took over this civilian merchant ship, and hijacked it.

What he did was piracy. But a great tolerance has grown up in the seafaring world about piracy. I think he took this ship in Brazilian waters. He thought that he would get help from Brazil, and he didn't get it.

Q: He was trying to stage a revolt against the dictator in Protugal.

Burke: Yes, Salazar. He did stage a revolt against Salazar. But he thought he would get help from Brazil because Brazil had been a Portuguese colony. But Brazil hadn't been a Portuguese colony for a long, long time, and he didn't recognize that they were really two separate countries, and there was only an emotional tie between Brazil and Portugal. They weren't going to do anything to really offend Portugal. So they were about to seize this ship, the civilians were, and he sailed, he went all around the seas trying to find a home, trying to find some place to go.

Well, we were in a quandary. I wanted to put out a great big search, because once a ship gets to sea it's not so easy to find as a lot of people think it is. But we couldn't do it. We dilly dallied before we finally made up our minds that we ought to know where that ship was. And piracy was piracy.

Q: Were we approached by the Portuguese government or by

the Brazilian government?

Burke: I don't know. I'm sure we were approached by the Portuguese government, but whether we were approached by the Brazilian government, we probably were by both of them but I don't know now, I've forgotten.

But anyway, finally we started the search, and it took us an ungodly long time to find them, because our people were out of the habit of conducting a search at sea. The aircraft squadrons hadn't been doing that in practice. Our search plans weren't very good. Our ships-- I don't think anybody in the Navy now understands the retiring search curve, or search from flank or search from ahead. But anyway, we didn't do a very good job on that. We finally located it.

Q: Then we trailed it for a while.

Burke: We trailed it for a while, that was what we wanted to do. We wanted to know what was happening so he would not violate any more laws of the sea, but neither could we--we could not take the ship away from him. Although that was proposed, too.

Q: Did you have any contact with this admiral?

Burke: Not after. Before I talked several times with him.

He was not bad. He had a lot of very fine ideas. The only thing was, a man's got to obey the laws of his country. You can't—he just got so frustrated, probably one of the early ones of forming a militant minority and thinking he could get away with it. Well, he couldn't. I don't know what happened to him. He later went to Brazil.

Q: Another incident of tremendous interest is the so-called Bay of Pigs incident. Would you talk about that?

Burke: No, there are two things that I never talk about. One of them is women, because I don't know enough about women, and the other one is the Bay of Pigs because I know too much about the Bay of Pigs.

Now, the reason for that is that the President required all reports of the Bay of Pigs to be submitted to him, and they're gone. What really happened in the Bay of Pigs that I can't prove and nobody else can either was a complete breakdown in governmental ability to take actions in a complex situation. Now, by that I mean that when the new administration came in, they wanted to do away with red tape. They didn't like the way government had been run. They didn't like the complicated, what they thought were delaying procedures that had been developed. And when Mr. Kennedy took office, he not only took office but he brought a great big team in, not just his Cabinet officers but also second, third and fourth echelon people, and placed them in various positions of government, and most of these people, nearly all of these people were ardent, enthusiastic people without any experience whatever in administering anything, including the President. He'd always been in Congress. He'd never had any sort of a job that required any administration.

None of the rest of them had either. So they didn't understand ordinary administrative procedures, the necessity for having lines of communication and channels of command. The President himself would pick up the telephone and call people who were not connected with an operation, and give them orders or instructions or ask advice. He did this with me lots of times, and at first I thought it was just a question of information, but later I found out that he never paralleled that by going down the chain of command, for example. And so I got in the habit, and so did the other Chiefs, when we got a telephone call from the President, we informed all the other people as soon as we could of what it was, so that they would be informed of it.

Well, there was a breakdown, a complete breakdown of channels, not only in the Bay of Pigs but every other way. There was a change of plans at the last minute. There was--

there were conflicting orders given to different people. There was an unreasonable amount of secrecy involved so that people who should have known about the operation didn't know it. There was not enough checking by anybody including the Chiefs. The Chiefs themselves did not realize how little the administration knew or how small their capability was for that kind of thing. And we didn't insist upon knowing. They would have told us probably, but we were not tough enough. Our big fault was standing in awe of the Presidency instead of pounding the table and demanding and being real rough, we were not. We set down our case and then we shut up and that was a mistake.

Their big mistake was that they didn't realize the tremendous importance of the operation or the effect it would have on the world. They didn't realize the power of the United States or how to use the power of the United States. It was a game to them. It was another election. They were inexperienced people.

I don't blame the President very much, except for his inability to choose people as advisors. It was a fiasco. But what I propose to do with the Bay of Pigs, I have very few papers, I have most everything I think that's been written about it, and someday I'm going to try to assemble all of the data and what few notes I have, my few personal notes, and try to get a sequence of events and what happened from what I know about it.

Now, the trouble is that there were a lot of orders given that I don't know anything about. That operation was not under the military. We were told that every time we got anywhere near it--we had no responsibility for it, we were not supposed to comment on things, unless we were asked to, it was not our show, it was a CIA operation and you stay the hell out of it, and we will not permit any regular force of the United States to become involved in this, and so you Chiefs cannot become involved.

Q: Was this the White House word?

Burke: This was the President himself. Every time. And it was repeated over and over again.

There was some truth to that. But it was a military operation which was conducted by amateurs, all, from top to bottom. And it was a horrible fiasco. The Chiefs' one error in that was that we did not--although the papers that we wrote said that the operation had a 50 percent chance of being successful, when the original landing place was Trinidad, I think it was Operation Trinidad, it had less chance of being successful when the Bay of Pigs was selected, which was required by the President. We said those things, but we didn't insist. We didn't pound the desk.

Other than that, I don't want to--

Q: How much in advance did the Chiefs know about this?

Burke: The operation? Not until after Kennedy was President, the planning--

Q: --the planning had been under way for a long time?

Burke: No, the planning had not been under way for a long time. This is one of the sad things about it, the planning-- the first time that I knew about that was when our Navy intelligence people uncovered some operations in Guatemala. So I knew that something was cooking. And then it was either just before the Inauguration in January that we were informed that there was going to be an operation, or just after the Inauguration, but in any case, we were not briefed on the operation. We had no idea of what kind of an operation it was until after the Inauguration. And even then we were given the rough plan, which was really just a synopsis of an operating plan, to comment on. And that's when we told the President, in writing with our endorsement on it, that we could not comment on the operation because it had no logistics annex and no communication annex and that sort of stuff, and we'd have to have that before, we'd have to know that situation before we could make any intelligent comment. But from the looks of the operating plan, we thought it had about a 50 percent chance of success, from Trinidad.

For example, my Vice Chief never knew about the Bay of Pigs. I was forbidden to tell him. So there was none of my staff knew anything about it.

Q: Did the Joint Chiefs have a chance to talk with Allen Dulles?

Burke: Yes, somewhat, mostly with (Richard) Bissel, and they would brief us. Allen Dulles was not feeling very well at the time and during the actual Bay of Pigs affair I think he was down in San Juan or some place. He was not in the States. Bissel and General Cabell were the ones who knew the details. They were both good people, but neither one--the CIA should not have tried to run that operation. Then it got big on them, that's what happened. It's like a lot of other things, it got bigger than they initially intended, expected, and got beyong their capacity to control.

It came very close to being successful, that operation, very close. A couple of little things could have happened. Or if a couple of things had not happened, it might have been a successful operation--it was so close.

Q: Success would have altered the history of the present day, wouldn't it?

Burke: Yes. It was so close. And this is true with many operations. There is a time when just a little extra push will make it work.

Q: This is where the professional know-how would have been valuable.

Burke: Yes. I wanted very much--did you ever read Mario Lazho's book?

Q: No.

Burke: You ought to read that book. He's got a lot in there that I never knew, and I don't know whether that is correct or not, but of the things that I know about, he's pretty close to the truth, on the thing. Of course, he's a Cuban.

Q: I hope, Admiral, that you will carry through on what you said and that you will someday write the account from your point of view for the Historical record, because after all--

Burke: I'm awfully lazy and I don't like to write. But I hope I will. There are several things I want to write about--the Bay of Pigs, the B-36 investigation, the Korean

Armistice. I've got a lot of notes on the Korean Armistice, notes on the war.

Q: In 1961, a very happy event--the GEORGE WASHINGTON completed her first voyage and completed it successfully, having been at sea for 66 days. This must have been the cause of some jubiliation for you.

Burke: You're certainly right. That was one program that went through without a hitch. No, that's not true--without any hitch that we couldn't overcome. When she was successful and on schedule and within her budget, all this whole program, and when everything worked so very well on the very first time, it was a source of great--a great load off my mind and an awful lot of other people's, a lot of people who really made that happen.

Especially, of course, because things had been going so smoothly, and being sort of cynical, based on a lot of experience, I thought surely something would go wrong, very wrong. But it didn't.

Q: You were on hand when she came to port, were you not?

Burke: Yes. I've forgotten where it was now. I think it was New London, I don't know. But that was a good thing for the country.

Q: And the Navy played it up, too.

Burke: Oh, yes. Oh, yes.

Q: That suggests something to me. In World War II and prior to World War II the Navy was really not concerned with public relations, but seemingly it learned fast in the post-war era. Do you want to comment on that and your role in this development?

Burke: Well, you are absolutely right. Before World War II, I don't suppose there were over three officers in Washington who were involved in public relations, and those were appointed primarily to keep public media people from bothering the officers. In other words, we didn't want any publicity. They were buffers. We didn't want any publicity, and we were taught when we were kids to keep our mouths shut, and that an officer who sought publicity or who got publicity was not the proper kind of an officer to be.

I remember that frequently people, naval officers had to make speeches, like Admiral Senn, Commander of the base force. He got all the pseeches because he was a good speaker and none of the other admirals would make a speech, so he got them all. But they said, "Poor old Admiral Senn, he's a good speaker, period." He wasn't, he was a pretty good naval officer.

During the war, Admiral Nimitz realized I suppose first that for the country to know, it couldn't depend on just handouts from the Navy Department. They were dull. Naval officers didn't know how to write the stuff up that was interesting. They left out all the things that would be of interest to readers, and they were dull facts. Also he had tremendous pressure from newspaper people to go out on the ships, and he succumbed to that after a while.

Q: Maybe with the aid of the Army and the Air Force, their efforts in that area.

Burke: Probably. Probably. He had to do it in self defense, he thought. But he asked the newspaper people not to violate security, to follow the security rules, and I remember the first time I ran into it was down at the Solomons there, where there were quite a few newspaper people who liked to ride with me, and they were always very good people. I never had any trouble. I couldn't censor their stuff, write ups. I didn't have time to fool with any censorship or determine what should or should not be written, but they always took it over to headquarters ashore some place and went over it with somebody, they never violated, and this was quite a few people.

Later when I became Chief of Staff to Admiral Mitscher,

everybody wanted to ride with him. He didn't want anything to do with it. He was a man who got a tremendous amount of very favorable publicity by trying to avoid all publicity. He didn't want them around. But they all wanted to be around him. He had a dry humor.

Q: You had your share of that, too, did you not? You were a colorful figure.

Burke: No. No. It was Admiral Mitscher. He was a hell of a sailor. He was good. And he was where the action was, but he made the action.

Q: I remember, '31 Knot Burke.'

Burke: That was before. But he had about 40 or 50 people, newspaper people, falling all over themselves on that carrier, and they too maintained--we had a censor aboard, but they were very good. Of course, they were trying, by that time they'd try to slip something in the mail or something like that, but usually the other people would find it out. But the newspaper people were extremely good.

Well, as a result of that, the newspaper people found that if they were where the action was, they could get some nice human interest stories, and this was in the days before they learned to distort it, and so after the war they wanted to continue that.

That, when unification came along, that was a very interesting episode, that created a lot of public interest. Then it became necessary for us to have a public relations department, in order to stay alive, to get money, to get recognition, to get the knowledge that your part of the service was an important part. So all the services started their public relations departments, started vying with each other. So now public relations is a very impatant aspect of what happens, of making decisions.

Q: It has grown increasingly with the development of communications in the country, radio, television--as a vehicle for public information.

Burke: Yes. I've tried to quit making speeches. I have a letter here on my desk, from Admiral Nimitz Center.

Q: In Fredericsburg, Texas?

Burke: Yes, down in Texas. They have written to me and said they have made arrangements for a television group, and this is all without me knowing anything about it, for an interview in the Washington area, on reminiscences of Admiral Nimitz. Well, I don't have many reminiscences of Admiral Nimitz, but at first I got awfully mad at this and said the hell with it, I'm not going to have anything to do with it. And yet it will do the Navy some good. It might be some good for history. Maybe I know something about Admiral Nimitz that other people won't bring out. So I'm going to say yes. I don't like it. It takes a lot of work.

This thing down at the Naval Academy here, Willie Mack asked me to come down to a seminar in April where he wants me to talk before the history division, I guess of the Naval Academy. I started to say no on that. But maybe there'll be some people down there who'll do some good, and maybe the work will be of a little bit of value. But mostly I say no.

Q: Admiral, this being intended for the Eisenhower Library and Columbia University, their Eisenhower Project, would you--if you have some personal recollections of the President, which might be worthy of keeping?

Burke: I doubt if they're worthy of keeping. I do have-- and I'd like to preface that I didn't know President Eisenhower before I became CNO. I'd met him perhaps once or twice. He didn't know me. I wasn't in favor of a military man being President, because--not for the normal reasons, not for the fear of a military man, but because he would have the fear of being a military man in the Presidency and wouldn't exercise the authority that he probably should exercise, or if he didn't have that fear then he would exercise too damned much.

And yet, in a very short while, I came to have tremendous admiration and I suppose the only real good word is love for a man who had great characteristics and yet who had frailities, who had faults, who was not omnipotent, was not even very brilliant, but he had a hell of a lot of character.

Now, this change (and it changed fast) came about just from listening to him when he was--for example, when I went in to see him when--for the first time he appointed me as CNO--he gave me the duties that he thought a Chief of Staff ought to have. I don't agree with what he told me exactly, but what impressed me was that he believed what he said. He wasn't telling me something he himself didn't believe. It wasn't a window dressing for the thing. He was trying to get across to me, and did, what he felt were my primary duties.

It's a sort of a sense that you get when you're talking with a man like that. I had the same thing with Truman. Tremendous admiration, so that if he would tell me to do something, that I didn't know anything about, I would do it without hesitation, because he--even though I would have an uneasy feeling that maybe it's not the right thing to do, but I would do it because he wouldn't ask me to do that if he didn't think it was right. And I might question his judgment but I'd never question his integrity.

Now, how do you get that way? How do you get a feeling for a man like that? What does he do to cause you to have a feeling like that for him? And I think it's mostly informal conversation on--well, on any subject, so that he gradually gets his views across and how he formed those views.

Eisenhower was kind of lazy. He wasn't a great hard-working man. But the man had integrity and he had good judgment, and he had high standards. That is the most important attribute a President can have. Most Presidents do have that. In any case, he did. He did.

Other little things--I learned not to drink more than one drink with him because his steward always loaded the drinks. He liked to serve old fashioneds and when you get an old fashioned, it was in a great big old fashioned--double, they were triple, I think--so I never finished an old fashioned, because I wanted to walk out, and wanted to think, and if there were important--well, he never drank before important things, but if I thought that maybe something might be discussed and no decisions made, even so, I was very careful to take ginger ale.

He could never understand why I didn't play golf, and now I don't understand why I don't either. He knew a lot about the Navy, without knowing why the Navy had to do things the way they did it, but he would listen, more than most Army officers would listen, to why you can't do certain things that are done habitually in the Army, why you can't do them in the Navy. And it was nice to find somebody who would listen. I don't think he ever understood some of it.

Q: I suppose his experience in Europe in joint command had something to do with this.

Burke: A great deal. I mean, he was chosen for that, to head the American Expeditionay Force, because he had those qualities, qualities of understanding.

I have--little things, like he raised his kids right. They're good. John Eisenhower--it's terrible to be the son of a famous father, and yet he did pretty well. And the grandchildren are good, too.

Q: Did you ever go with him where it was just sheer relaxation? Did you ever go to Augusta with him?

Burke: I didn't go with him, because I was not a golfer,

and he liked to play golf. Some of the other chiefs did. Twining did, a little bit, but mostly we went down to Augusta--that is I think Twining did, I'm not really sure-- mostly we went down to Augusta for working sessions, go down to brief him or to submit our views on various things. He'd send for us. We would go to Augusta, and went out to Colorado I think twice, various other places where he would go. But we'd go swimming with him sometimes. Sometimes we'd go swimming in the White House. With Truman, too. Truman used to swim. We'd watch the movies once in a while. But mostly when we were with him informally, it was just a little while, never on any extended period, and that's wise--the President should steer clear of too close contact with his military, and yet be close enough to them so that he knows what the hell they think.

Q: Were you ever with him in Newport when he went up there in the summer time?

Burke: Yes. I went up there, not with him, I went up there at the same time he did once. I think that was because he went up there just before the spring conference, the Three Power Conference he had, and we saw him up there. We arranged the house for him. But most Presidents are wise in having some sort of civilian cronies to go with them, somebody who doesn't want anything, doesn't have any responsibility, that he can completely relax with.

See, one of the things that I don't forgive Max Taylor for is that Max used some of the material in his book, was derived from a very informal conversation, where the President wasn't thinking of how that could be used, and Max used it. And that's bad. The President never intended what Max thought he implied or intended.

Q: A President is entitled to periods when he can relax and know that he's not being quoted.

Burke: Yes, he's got to have that. A man's got to have that. This is why Nixon has Rebosa and why Truman had his people.

Q: I know that Admiral George Miller, who was very close to you, worked for a long time under your supervision when you were CNO. He has developed certain ideas in the realm of national defense. And I suspect that they probably reflect your thinking in large measure. Would you talk about this?

Burke: Yes. When I first became CNO, one of the things that I realized even before was that it was very difficult for a civilian or for another service to understand just what significance the Navy is to the power of the nation.

Nations have lost their existence because they didn't understand the importance of seapower. Nations that understood it have lost because they didn't know how to use seapower. They didn't know--The control of the sea, and the maintenance of communications, sea communications, is a necessity for an important nation. Somebody--it's a necessity for any nation, only for a small nation, other people can control it and let them in on it.

Now, after I realized that this was a big gap in our educational requirements, that we had to educate people and it had to be done with truth, it had to be done with real research, real examples, and there couldn't be any just emotional froth in it, I established a section called 0 9 (dog)--I'm surprised I remember. And 0 9 (dog) was given a responsibility for developing the basis for explaining seapower to everybody, including the Navy.

Well, I've gotten some very good people in that over the years. I've forgotten who it was that started it, but there was Jack McCain, George Miller, Hank Miller, a whole lot of people had gone through that mill, and they did a magnificent job.

Now, what is it? Why is it that seapower is so important? Is it really important? Haven't things changed over the generations? It's true that the Mediterranean, control of the Mediterranean has always been a necessity for any Mediterranean power to become a great power of the Mediterranean. Turkey was a powerful nation as long as it had a navy, and when she lost it she lost everything. Now, did the loss of the navy come first or did she lose something else and then lose the navy? Britain was powerful for centuries, when she had control of the sea. China in the very early days was most important when her junks plied to the Middle East, and then when they didn't do that, when she forgot that, they became a landlocked nation. Germany lost two world wars because she never understood how to control the sea, and she came awfully close to it, but she didn't grasp the necessity for the continued action of the slow throttling of a nation by blockade, by taking their merchant ships little by little--there's no one spectacular action that causes them to lose, it's a whole series of consecutive actions. Every time it costs them so much that they can't bear the cost eventually.

Well, that lesson has been lost in history over and over again, and it's lost right now, it's lost, although Zumwalt is doing one hell of a good job in explaining that. Most everything that Admiral Zumwalt does, I disagree with, but he does that extremely, extremely well.

Now, you don't have to have a tremendously large navy, I mean an overwhelmingly large one. What you have to have primarily are the naval people who can use their initiative, to carry out the policy of their government, both in peace and in war. This means training of people within the Navy. But first it means you've got to have a policy, a governmental policy to use not only the Navy but all the powers that a nation must have and must use in order to remain powerful, or not only remain powerful, in order to have an influence on future events in the world.

Well, that means the people in the Navy had to understand it. So Op 9 (dog) put out information within the Navy, on showing the flag, on the importance of the Navy under various conditions, why you had to have a Navy before you could have any expedition overseas, because you couldn't support any operation overseas for any significant length of time without control of the seas--why it was that the Soviet Union did not have to control the seas, because she is a land power, she has to deny us control; why it was that we had to have carriers until we could find some other way of protecting our sea lines, not just to protect the carriers or to fly airplanes over a nation, but in order to protect the damn merchantships, which was the backbone of the thing. And why it was it you wanted to land some place you had to have an amphibious force, to land against the will of the people who are there if that becomes necessary. Why submarines were so important and why, if you put ballistic missiles at sea, since you didn't know where they were, nobody knew where they were, they were not vulnerable--why they became invulnerable at sea, at least until somebody got an anti-submarine capability that nobody now has. Why it was that speed is important at sea, and turn around time, and all of these things that George has--he didn't get from me. He got them from a lot of people who were studying this problem. No nation in history has really been great as a world-wide power until they had control of the sea, or until they could assure that what they needed from the sea, they got. This is what Russia found out in the Cuban missile crisis, when I think that Khrushchev had no idea that he could really establish those missiles in Cuba and keep him there. I think that what he did have an idea was that he had his hand on the control rods all the time and that if, under the very best circumstances for Russia, that if the United States had no guts whatever, then--and if he could keep those missiles in Cuba and flaunt them at the United States, it wasn't because of the military capability of those missiles, which would be considerable, but that wasn't it, it was because he could demonstrate that the United States had lost its will to stand up to anything and that everybody could push them around. If he could win that, which I don't think he could ever have expected to win, he would have taken over the world in one fell swoop. But if he didn't do that, he could at least keep Cuba free of American domination. Cuba had gone Communist. There was a danger it was going to slip away, from uprisings and from other Latin American countries.

Q: And I suppose the Bay of Pigs taught him that.

Burke: And the Bay of Pigs. So he wanted to keep Cuba under Comminist domination, so--they've never lost a nation once they've taken over. So at the worst he could get that. And he knew damn well that he didn't have the missile power, that Russia didn't have the missile power compared to the United States, so if it came to a showdown, and there would be an exchange of missiles, Russia would have been destroyed and the United States would not have been badly hurt. He knew that we knew it, too. So I don't think he had any idea of a nuclear confrontation ever. But what he missed was that in spite of having all the studies that they had made, and all the words that they had spoken about the importance of seapower, he never realized the importance of power at sea, and how helpless he was when he was confronted with one American destroyer that said, "turn this ship around." There wasn't a damn thing he could do. He could storm and rave and threaten, but if that destroyer had the guts to make it happen, they would either sink the ship or the God damned ship would turn around.

Now, this is what jolted him. It really jolted him, I think. So that was in '62. So they decided then that they not only had to have a nuclear capability, which they were desperately working on to equal ours or better it, but they also had to have--and the was the first time that they ever, in spite of all their studying and reading of the effects of war, did they every really realized what a navy was all about. So they started.

Q: Practical experience.

Burke: Yes, he got his nose rubbed into it, practically. So by 1966 they had developed a good navy, and this is why they are now putting such tremendous emphasis on it.

Well, this is what George Miller knows. This is what all the people who went through this 0 9 (dog) business know, because they were working on the thing.

Now, how do you explain all of the possible circumstances? This is why George goes after the surface effect ships, the SES type and hydrofoils, and he's--I just won a dollar from him. Ten years ago he bet me a dollar or a drink or something that by 1973 we would have a hundred-knot ship. And I told him it wouldn't happen so soon. I called him up and reminded him of that one--on my check off sheet he said he'd pay it.

Side 2

Q: The Russians for some time have had an understanding of the value of a merchant fleet that we have not had, apparently. Where does that enter into this picture?

Burke: Well, seapower is composed of many different things. One of them is knowledge of currents, knowledge of ships, knowledge of sea bottoms, knowledge of sonar conditions--in other words, sea knowledge. The next one is fish. There's a lot of fish in the sea and fish is very important and getting more important, and not only are the fish important but the fishermen are import--they know where the fish are and they can learn a tremendous lot of things about that. The next, the merchantmen are the base for the whole thing. Merchant ships carry the goods, and 95 percent of the goods of the world are carried by ships, maybe more. In peace time we form relationships with people to whom we ship. A nation forms commercial relationships. They're not as important as some people have said they are, but they're of some importance. In any case, merchant ships plying into a nation's harbor learn an awful lot about the nation. The nation, if it's handled properly, a nation can become dependent upon another nation's merchant marine, and this Russia knows--that is straight economics among other things. So she developed a merchant marine first.

There's another reason for developing a merchant marine first and that's because she had not had any real high seas sailors ever, or for a long, long time, and you help develop those by sending your people to sea in merchant ships just so they can learn that the ocean is big and powerful.

Then, of course, there's the navy, that is supposed to support our merchantmen, supposed to support our fishermen, supposed to do research and support other oceangraphic research,--we have forgotten within the Navy, the Navy has now forgotten that one of our missions, one of its missions is to support merchant marine. So has the merchant marine. They went different ways, and the Navy knows very little about our merchant marine now or the importance of a merchant marine, and the marchant marine knows very little about our Navy now. The same thing is true of fishermen. There could well be established within the Navy a small group of people that know a great deal about fishermen and fishing, and how to help our fishermen, and vice versa. But there is very little connection. And I tried to establish that when I was CNO, unsuccessfully.

Q: How did you attempt to go about it?

Burke: Talked to fishing groups. But you see the fishing groups, the canneries and the trawlers are owned by separate groups and there's no big group of people that you can talk to that will be helpful. The same thing is true with our merchant marine. The merchant marine is divided in many different ways--subsidized, unsubsidized, passenger, just freight, various companies, scheduled liners, unscheduled. Our unions versus our management.

But we are in a very bad way now for our total seapower, as George has undoubtedly emphasized. He's sponsoring seapower now. He's correct in saying that we don't recognize our merchant marine. He is incorrect I think is some of the reasons for that. He says that--he thinks that management has a greater control--the management of merchant marine elements have greater control over their destiny than they actually do have. The merchant marine is an economic monster and it must do things which are economical, on which they can make a small profit-or they don't stay in existence. They go broke. And they have gone broke, company after company after company has gone broke. A good deal of that is caused because our shipbuilding costs are high, very much higher than foreign costs. Labor on US flagships is much more expensive than foreign seamen. Not only on direct pay, but the perquisites, the food, the living quarters, the time off.

For example, I made a cruise on a Grace Liner where the second assistant or assistant engineer made a great deal more money total than I made as Chief of Naval Operations, because he got time and a half, he got a high salary in the first place, he got a bonus, he got time and a half or double time, overtime pay when he worked more than so many hours per day. He got a tremendous amount of leave or he got extra pay when he didn't use the leave. But he ended up with an annual take-home pay of a tremendous amount, I think it was something on the order of nearly $40,000.

Well, they priced us out of ordinary people being able to ship, on American ships. George says that people ought to ship American, which they should, but you can't expect an American company to ship American when it costs twice as much or a considerable amount more, which may be the whole profit margin, than if you ship on a foreign ship.

So you have to start way back. George doesn't want

to start way back. He wants to do it now all at once. Well, it probably can't be done that way. It would be nice if it could. He says that our shipbuilding costs are coming down. They are, comparatively, not because ours are coming down but because foreign yards are going up. But still, although we build better ships probably than any place else in the world, it's still more expensive.

Now, if you're going to run a commercial operation, such as fishing, our fishing industry is suffering the same way. Foreign fishermen can deliver fish, canned fish to St. Louis, cheaper than we can deliver it to St. Louis because of the cost of trawlers, the cost of canning, the cost of labor. And perhaps more efficient because they're struggling harder.

Q: They're not concerned about the eight hour day.

Burke: Not so much as we are, in any case. But all this is part of sea power.

Q: The Russians have a distinct advantage because their merchant merine, I believe, is a component part of their navy, is it not?

Burke: No, it's not really a component part of the navy, but--that's an advantage in a ways. But supposing our merchant marine was a part of our Navy right now. It wouldn't be any advantage to our merchant marine. It's because they recognize the importance of their merchant marine all the way through, by their navy and by the civilian hierarchy. They've got it. They learned that the hard way. Unless we change our ideas, we're going to learn it the hard way some day when we're suddenly stopped from doing something, like not having fuel, and we can't do anything about it. And it's a desperate move which may or may not be successful, because we will have forgotten how to use naval power for that.

Q: During the time that you were CNO, the idea was suggested, I don't think it got very far, that perhaps merchant men at sea might be a place to put missiles for the defense of the nation.

Burke: Sure.

Q: Were you back of this idea?

Burke: I was. I thought it would be a very good thing, because you could put half a dozen missiles on a merchant ship and let her ply her regular trade, and have a small naval contingent aboard ready, and it would be just like a submarine. You could handle it all right. But it would be complicated and nobody wanted to do it.

Q: Was it not also an effort to upgrade the status of the merchant marine.

Burke: No.

Q: That was not a factor?

Burke: No. It wouldn't have been a factor. It would have interferred with the merchant marine to some extent because it would have taken part of their cargo hold and they'd have had to feed people and stuff like that. But it could have been done.

Q: It certainly would have made the Navy as a whole more aware of the merchant marine.

Burke: Yes.

Q: When Hank Miller was in Op 9 (dog) he said when he arrived, he and the others were ordered by you to produce a naval plan for the Eisenhower Administration which had just come in. He said you ordered this accomplished in ten days.

Burke: They were able to do that in ten days.

Q: Was your thinking as developed as it is now, in terms of the value of seapower?

Burke: Oh, yes. Oh, yes, probably more so then, and all the data was there. You see, the trouble with naval officers and all military people, in common with a lot of other people, is that a plan doesn't have to be voluminous. It can be very short and concise and very good. It doesn't have to weigh ten tons. But no planner ever really thought this out.

Q: Was this something you instigated on your own, or was President Eisenhower interested in a new fresh approach?

Burke: Well, I think--of course, every incoming administration always wants to change everything that the other administration has done, and they always want a fresh approach. But in addition to that, it's good to re-survey your situation, your own situation, every once in a while, to make sure that you're on the right track and that you're not going to goof over something. You take your own financial situation. Now, probably about once a year you take a look and see, how am I doing and what have I done wrong, and you find a lot of things that you've just been sitting on and not doing, that you could have done, and you change. You've got to re-examine what you're doing periodically. And this was primarily what--you get so you hear stale words but you don't understand them any more. So if you can re-word even the same thing, it brings a better understanding.

Q: When you took this plan to the President, which I assume you did, what was his reaction?

Burke: Well, he thought of it as just another one of these Navy attempts, I think, but he paid attention. He paid attention.

You see, I always had trouble because I didn't want to be spectacular. This is one of the things I have a little trouble with George on. George wants to go farther than I would want to go. He overstates, I think. I like to understate. He may be stating it right on and I want to understate.

But if you call "wolf, wolf," then you can be in trouble some day. If you understate you can also be in trouble, but it's not so big a problem.

Q: You always have some place to go.

Burke: Yes, and this is why--it might have been better if I had made, gone the full limit on what I could have said about seapower, with justification but not so much justification. There is a need for a damn good Army and a damn good Air Force, too. And you can't just fight all out for a Navy.

You've got to have some sort of balance, and everybody's idea of what that balance is will be different.

Q: I want to thank you very much for this series. I think it's been vastly interesting, and for the record quite valuable.

Admiral Burke: I thank you very much.

INDEX

FOR

INTERVIEWS WITH

ADMIRAL ARLEIGH A. BURKE,
U. S. NAVY (RETIRED)

Amity Cruises: 188-189

Arctic SS expeditions: 147-149, 152, 157

Aswan Dam: see entries under Suez Canal.

Bay of Pigs: 175; Burke's comments, 216-222

Bissel, Richard M.: 221

Bridges, The Hon. H. Styles: Senator from New Hampshire, 171-172

Brinkmanship: comments on use of power in dealing with other nations, 37 ff, 70

Brown, Adm. Charles R. (Cat): 86-87

Burke, Admiral Arleigh A.: appointment as CNO, 6-9; his attitude towards his appointment, 8-10; as Captain serves on General Board, 10-12; his attitude towards an understudy for CNO, 12; problem in naming his successor in 1961, 13-15; tours Far East before taking over as CNO, 16-18; struggle over question of dependence on draft vs. volunteer service, 28-34; Eisenhower uses Burke as sounding board for various subjects, 34-36, 79-80, 84; comments on brinkmanship and use of power, 38 ff; affair in Lebanon, 44-46; Suez crisis, 46-48; Burke on B-50 bomber, 58-60; reliance on Vice Chief for detailed work, 62-63; Burke's concept of VCNO who would disagree with him, 62-65; Burke in South Pacific, meets with Whizzer White, his first experience with a staff member who could and did oppose him on certain occasions, 66; on R and D program, 73-74; Burke's position on bringing troops home from Europe, 83-85; orders 6th fleet on alert at time of Suez crisis, 86-88; Burke on guided missile work, 88 ff; comments on research projects and need for selected personnel, 94-95; on missile gap - intelligence interpretation, 97-99; illustration of point on intelligence interpretation, 98-100; his attitude towards taking away from CNO command of fleets, 107-111; opinion on DEW Line, 120-121; Burke on secrecy, 154-155; difficulties while serving on Korean Military Armistice Commission, 162 ff; Burke on right strategy in S. Vietnam, 173-175; various projects undertaken with foreign navies, 189-191; relationships with foreign naval personages, 192 ff; reappointment in 1959, 207-210; summary of his feelings for President Eisenhower, 228-231

Cabell, Gen. Charles P., USAF: 221

Carney, Adm. Robert B.: 6-7; sends Burke on tour of Far East prior to duties as CNO, 16-18; recommendations on volunteer service, 29

Centralization in the Services: 105-107; Burke's convictions contrary to those of President Eisenhower, 107-111; 114-115; downgrading of SecNav, 114-116

CIA: in Laos, 178, 180

USS CONSTITUTION: fire in her while building in Brooklyn Navy Yard, 211-213

Conventional Weapons System: 51-52

Cuban Missile Crisis: 23 ff; provides watershed in development of Russian naval power, 25

Defense Department reorganization: amendments to National Defense Act 1958, 102-105

DEW Line: Early Warning System, 118-120

Diem, Ngo Dinh, President of South Vietnam: 19; 168-169; 173-174

Dulles, The Hon. Foster: Secretary of State, discussion of Dulles and use of power, 37 ff; Suez crisis, 46; Dulles and massive retaliation, 51 ff; 86

Duncan, Adm. Donald B.: (Wu), first VCNO to Admiral Burke, 62

Ecuadorian Naval Academy: 182-186

Eden, The Hon. Anthony: Prime Minister at time of Suez crisis, 47-48

Eisenhower, President Dwight D.: Burke's first meeting, 1; Eisenhower's concept of use of CVs, 1-3; 13; President stresses to Burke importance of his job as member of Joint Chiefs, 21-22; his desire to have Joint Chiefs reach agreement on problems, 22, 55-61; his ability to make objective decisions when dealing with military services, 26-28; incident involving Burke and the President over the subject - the draft vs volunteer service, 28-34; Eisenhower uses Burke as sounding board on various subjects, 34-36; also 79-84; incident over U.S. plane shot down off China coast, 42-44; Eisenhower and Lebanon affair, 45-46; Eisenhower and Massive Retaliation, 51 ff; the President and Conventional Weapons systems, 51 ff; more on conventional weapons, 69-70; appreciation of awesomeness of nuclear power, 69; Eisenhower concern about taxation and economic issues, 81-83; his concern in making good appointments, 83; Eisenhower asks Congress for a mandate to reorganize the Defense Department, 103; his understanding of the use of national power, 144-145; reluctance to authorize Arctic expedition, 150-151; his determination not to commit forces on mainland in SE Asia, 168; convinces Burke it was his duty to stay on as CNO, 210

Egyptian aid: 81

Felt, Adm. H. D.: named by Burke as VCNO, talent for disagreeing with CNO in constructive manner, 63-65; named CinCPac (1958), 64-65

Foreign Aid: for Ecuador, 182-186; Ethiopia, 186; requests for warships, 186

Galvao, Adm. H. Malta: hijacks (1961) Portugese passenger ship in Atlantic, 213-215

General Board - Navy: Burke serves there as Captain, 10; efforts at bringing in problems for discussion, 11-12

USS GEORGE WASHINGTON: her launching in 1961, 223

German Navy: help for fledgling post-war navy, 199-200

Greek Navy: 203-204

Guayaquil: location of Ecuadorian Naval Academy, 182

Guerrilla Warfare: 180-181

Guided Missiles: 88 ff; 101

Hamlet Program: 181

Hodge, Lt. Gen. John R.: Member, Military Armistice Commission in Korea (1951), 162-163

Holloway, Adm. James: Chief of Bureau of Personnel, 29-30

Holy Loch, Scotland: 135-136, 138-139; see also entries under POLARIS bases.

Hoshina, Adm.: prime mover in setting up new navy for Japan after WW II, 201-202

Hungnan, Korea: evacuation of, 99

International Relations: Burke and foreign navies, 182 ff

Japanese Navy: aid for her post-war (WWII) Navy, 201-202

Johnson, The Hon. Lyndon: President of the U.S. - agrees with Burke on tactics for Laos (1961), 171

Joint Chiefs of Staff: Eisenhower's concept of their functions, 21-22; difficulties in arriving at decision when money for services is involved, 23; further discussion of decision making and President's attitude, 55-61; 109-110; early attitude towards Arctic expedition, 150; role in Bay of Pigs affair, 217-221

Kennedy, The Hon. John F.: wants Burke to stay on as CNO, 13-14; briefing on situation in Laos - advice of Burke, 169; invites Burke to present his views before Congressional leaders, 169 ff; Burke's interpretation of Kennedy's policies in Vietnam, 173-175

Khrushchev, Nikita: Russian Communist party secretary, 237-238

Korean Military Armistice Committee: 162

Korean War: interpretation of intelligence, 98-99; Burke ascribes Korean war as the most direct reason for our involvement in SE Asia, 158-159; resume of the Korean War, 159-161

Kubitschek, Juscelino: President of Brazil (1956), 196-198

Laos: summary of our involvement in Laos, 165-167; Burke' presentation on Laos before President Kennedy and Congressional leaders, 169 ff; CIA in Laos, 178

Lebanon Affair: 45-46, 109

Lodge, The Hon. John: Ambassador to Spain, 127

Malta: possible base for POLARIS, 126

Mao-Tse-tung: his principles of war, 177

U.S. Marine Corps: in jeopardy in 1958 reorganization, 111-112

Massive Retaliation, statement of: 49-51

Matioso Maia: Brazilian Minister of the Navy, 187; 195-198

McLean, Dr. William: develops SIDEWINDER, 90-91

Miller, RADM George: 233-234, 239, 243-244

MINAS GERAS: Brazilian Aircraft Carrier, 187

Missile Gap: 96-99; 101

Missiles on Merchantmen: Burke backs this idea, 245

Mitscher, Adm. Marc A.: recommends Burke for promotion to flag rank, 8-9; attitude towards the press, 225-226

Mountbatten, Adm. Lord Louis: Suez crisis, 47; 127; his role in acquiring Polaris SSs for Britain, 139 ff; visit to Burke, 192-193

USS MUGFORD: 154-156

NATO Military Mission: 121-123

USS NAUTILUS: 147, 153, 156

U. S. Naval Academy: employment of Mexican instructor, 189-190

Naval Aviation: problems in 1958 reorganization of Defense, 113-114, 116

Navy Public Relations: 224; Burke's review of developing appreciation in navy for public relations, 224-228

Nimitz, Flt. Adm. Chester: 8-9

Nomura, Adm.: 201-202

POLARIS Submarines: Britain acquires some from U.S., 141-143

POLARIS Submarine Bases: 125; background to selection of Rota and Holy Loch, 125-126; present need, 137-139

Queen Fredericka: incident at Observatory Circle, 203-204; dinner on the West Coast, 206-207

Quemoy-Matsu: offshore islands, 38; 42-44, 109

Radford, Adm. Arthur: his attitude towards Navy when he served as Chairman of Joint Chiefs, 25-27

REGULUS I: 89

REGULUS II: 91; Russians use idea to develop the STIX, 93

R and D Program, Navy: (Research and Development), 73-74

Research Projects, Navy: 93-95

Rojectvensky, Adm. (Rozhdestvenski): Russian Admiral loses battle of Tsushima Strait, 1905, 24

Rota: 126-127; 129-130; justification for Rota, 130-131; opposition, 132-133; arrangements on sovereignty, 134-135

Ruge, Adm. R. (German): 190, 199; professor at University of Tubingen, 200

Russell, Adm. James S.: succeeds Adm. Felt as VCNO under Adm. Burke, 65

SS SANTA MARIA: Portugese passenger ship, hijacked by Adm. Galvao and Gen. Delgado, 213

Sarit Thanarat, Field Marshal: Premier of Thailand, 19

Seapower: Russians learn about seapower during Cuban Missile Crisis, 23-24; 37 ff; 40 ff; British understanding and use of seapower, 139-141; 233-248; Burke's concepts implemented when he becomes CNO, 233-234; sets up Op 09 to sell idea of seapower, 234-235; more on Soviets and Seapower, 236-238; importance of merchant ships in the picture, 240-241; fishermen, 240-241

SIDEWINDER: air to air missile developed at Inyokern, 90-91

Southeast Asian Involvement: 158 ff; Laos, 165 ff; South Vietnam, 168 ff

Stump, Adm. Felix: 19; Burke's estimate of him, 20

TALOS: 89

Taylor, General Maxwell: 27

TERRIER: 89

Tetrahedrons: used in construction of breakwater for Rota, 131-132

Thomas, The Hon. Charles: Secretary of the Navy, 7, 31; involvement with Burke over difference of opinion on draft vs volunteer service, 31 ff; 36-37

Truman, President Harry S.: 164

Twining, General Nathan: dealing with him as Chairman of JCS, 26

VANGUARD I: initial missile in orbit, 101-102

Vietnam: 74-78; enemy misreads temper of U.S., 146; Burke's discussion of our involvement, 173 ff; Kennedy failure to carry through on Vietnam, 175; threat of Chinese involvement, 176-177

Volunteers - for military service: debate over this, 28-34

White, Justice Byron R. (Whizzer): joins Burke's staff in South Pacific, assigned role of critic, 65-66-67-68

Willoughby, Major Gen. Charles A.: G-2 for Gen. MacArthur in Korea, 98-100